The Practical Handbook of
PAINTING
AND
WALLPAPERING

By Morton Shultz

Fawcett Publications, Inc.
67 West 44th Street
New York, New York 10036

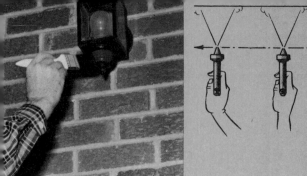
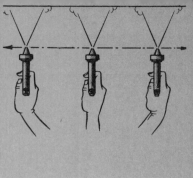

LARRY EISINGER: *Editor-in-Chief*

GEORGE TILTON: *Executive Editor*

SILVIO LEMBO: *Creative Director* • HAROLD E. PRICE: *Associate Director*

RAY GILL: *Editor*

ELAINE SAPOFF: *Production Editor* • ALAINE TROW: *Production Assistant*

Editorial Staff: JOE PIAZZA, DAN BLUE, FRANK BOWERS,
ELLENE SAUNDERS, PAMELA RIDDLE, AMY MORRIS

Art Staff: MIKE GAYNOR, ALEX SANTIAGO, JOHN SELVAGGIO,
HERBERT JONAS, JOHN CERVASIO, JACK LA CERRA

How-To Art by Henry Clark
Cover Color from The Sherwin-Williams Co.

Printed in U.S.A. by
FAWCETT-HAYNES PRINTING CORPORATION
Rockville, Maryland

CONTENTS

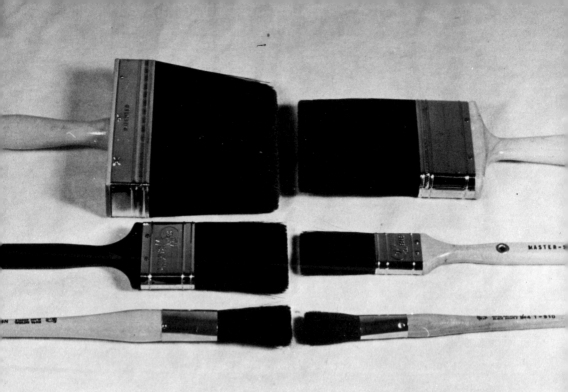

Paint brush styles. Row on left (from bottom to top) shows a #8 oval sash-and-trim brush, a 3″ varnish brush, and a 7″ calcimine brush. Row on right (from bottom to top) shows a #4 oval sash-and-trim, a 1½″ flat sash-and-trim, and a 4″ wall brush.

PAINT BRUSHES

A high quality brush should cost as much as a gallon of paint

It may seem like a conflict of thought that a book whose main theme is painting should have paint brushes, rather than paint, as the topic of its first chapter. The reason for this is that paint applicators, whether brush, roller or spraying equipment, must meet certain quality standards before you can achieve a good paint job. Even the most expensive paint, if applied with a shoddy, inexpensive paint brush, will give less than acceptable results.

Conversely, a good brush spreads paint evenly and leaves no glaring brush marks or loosened bristles on the surface. It is easy to handle, doesn't pull, and you can keep cleaning and re-using if for many years. A high quality paint brush should cost you almost as much as a gallon of high quality paint.

What is meant by a high quality paint brush? The finest ones use 100 percent nylon as the filament or pure natural bristles of which hog hair is best. Nylon

Surface or Object to be Painted		Brush to Use
Large exterior and interior surfaces—		Wall brush. A calcimine brush, if you can handle it, is particularly useful for painting exterior surfaces, such as a home's siding.
Asbestos wall	Floors	
Boats	Interior walls	
Ceilings	Roofs	
Cinder or cement block	Shingles	
Clapboard	Stone	
Concrete walls	Stucco	
Decks	Swimming pools	
Medium size areas—		Larger varnish or flat sash-and-trim brushes for flat surfaces. Oval sash-and-trim brushes of #8, #10, or #12 size for irregular surfaces.
Baseboards	Large windows	
Cabinets	Picket fences	
Cupboards	Rainspouts	
Doors	Shutters	
Eaves	Small boats	
Gutters	Steps	
Large pipes	Tabletops	
Small, narrow, or corner areas—		Small varnish or flat sash-and-trim brushes for flat surfaces. Oval sash-and-trim brushes of #2, #4, or #6 size for irregular surfaces.
Chairs	Screens	
Garden tools	Scrollwork	
Ladders	Small pipes	
Metal furniture	Trellises	
Radiators	Windows	

You need both a quality paint brush and a quality paint to assure a really good job.

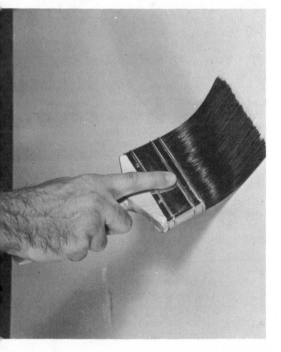

filament brushes can be used with any type of paint, including water-emulsion and oil base paints. Natural bristle brushes should be used *only* with oil-base paint, varnish, shellac, and lacquer.

Never use a natural bristle brush in a water-emulsion paint. Bristles absorb water like a blotter. They become sloppy, destroying their ability to spread paint evenly and smoothly.

When you go to buy paint brushes, there are three things to consider: style, size, and physical characteristics. Style and size allow you to select the one brush best suited for the job you are doing. Physical characteristics allow you to distinguish a good brush from one that is cheaply made. The following is a discussion of these considerations:

STYLES AND SIZES

There are four styles that will concern you. They are wall brushes (of which a calcimine brush is one type), varnish brushes, flat sash-and-trim brushes, and oval sash-and-trim brushes.

Varnish brushes useful when painting areas from 2" to 4" in size—such as on shutters.

A 4" wall brush is most comfortable to use for painting inside and outside of house.

National Paint, Varnish and Lacquer Association

Wall brushes come in 3 1/2", 4", and 5" widths. They are designed to hold a great quantity of paint for the painting of large flat areas, such as walls and ceilings. Calcimine (or block) brushes come in 6", 7", and 8" sizes and hold still more paint, but most homeowner-painters find them difficult to maneuver.

The size wall brush you select depends entirely on you. Pick one that feels comfortable, and one that you won't get tired wielding. In most cases, the ideal size for a home handyman is one of 4".

Varnish brushes are made in 2", 2 1/2", and 3" sizes. They are used for painting smaller flat surfaces, such as cabinets, baseboards, and moldings. They have a chisel trim which allows you to more easily cut the brush in at corners and baseboards. A chisel trim means that the tips of the filaments or bristles are beveled.

The size varnish brush you select is one that is small enough to get into the tightest spot you are painting, but wide enough to quickly cover the area. This is true as well for selection of flat sash-and-trim brushes.

Flat sash-and-trim brushes are made in 1", 1 1/2", and 2" sizes. They are designed primarily for painting narrow sash and trim, such as at windows. These are similar to varnish brushes, except that they don't have a chisel trim.

However, there is one type of sash brush which has its elements cut at an angle. These are called angular sash brushes and allow more uniform contact with a surface than a regular sash brush, with less chance of overlapping onto a surface you don't want painted. This makes them particularly useful when painting around window sash and door trim.

Oval sash-and-trim brushes are sized #2 (the smallest), #4, #6, #8, #10, and #12 (the largest). They are used for painting irregular and curved surfaces such as rounded furniture legs, pipes,

E.I. duPont de Nemours Co.

E.I. duPont de Nemours Co.

and scrollwork. The denser elements of these brushes and their shape allow coverage of ridges and rounds that would cause the elements of a flat brush to separate.

The accompanying chart, which summarizes what brushes to use for various circumstances, will guide you in selecting the right brush for the job you're doing.

PHYSICAL CHARACTERISTICS

There are four ways of distinguishing a good paint brush from a bad one. They are as follows:

● Full-bodied filaments or bristles of different lengths. The brush should feel full, not skimpy. Over half of the bristles or filaments should be of full brush length. The remainder should be in varying lengths to allow the brush to carry a full load of paint and release it gradually rather than in a glob. Inexpensive brushes have most elements the same length.

● If you are buying a nylon brush, each filament should be either tipped or flagged. If flagged, the filament is split at the tip. If tipped, the filament comes to a taper. At least 50 percent of the filaments of a good quality nylon brush are flagged, while the others are tipped.

● A good quality brush is clean. Dust and dirt should not fly from the brush as you strike it across your hand.

● A good paint brush has a sturdy handle made of beech, birch, hard maple, or plastic. The handle is balanced and should feel comfortable as you grasp it. The metal band that holds the elements, called the ferrule, should be made of corrosion-resistant stainless steel or copper.

THE RIGHT PRICE

About price, only guidelines can be offered. A good quality nylon wall brush costs from $8 to $10. A high quality pure bristle brush runs about $20. The huge difference between the two results from

The oval sash-and-trim brush is used mostly for painting round and irregular surfaces.

the fact that the highest quality bristle used in brushes originally came from China. It is now extremely difficult to get.

There is one time when you should not use an expensive paint brush. Some materials you spread with a brush contain chemicals that destroy elements; for example, muriatic acid for cleaning and etching masonry, epoxy resin paint, and liquid compounds needed for adhering fiberglass to a surface. These chemicals can't be cleaned from a brush. Therefore, when they are employed, it is best to use the least expensive paint brush you can buy and discard it after use.

Conversely, many people believe that you should use an inexpensive brush for applying shellac, varnish, and lacquer. This is not true for the same reasons that you shouldn't use an inexpensive brush for applying paint. Shellac, varnish, and lacquer can easily be cleaned from a good quality brush.

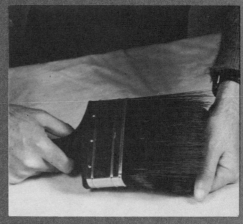

You can determine quality brushes by their bristles. They should be full, not skimpy.

Another sign of a high quality paint brush is that its bristles are of varying lengths.

When you strike filaments of good brush across your hand, no dust will fly from it.

A brush comb is very handy to have. Use it to straighten the elements after cleaning.

BRUSH PREPARATION

Before using a new paint brush for the first time, it should be cleaned to assure that no foreign matter embedded in the bristles or filaments will dirty the paint. Before using a new organic bristle brush, suspend it in linseed oil for at least 12 hours. Make sure the bristling doesn't rest on the bottom of the can. This will cause bristles to bend out of shape. One way to avoid this possibility is to extend a rod or dowel across the top of the can and hang the brush from it by drilling a hole through the handle.

After removing the brush from linseed oil, use a straight stick or a paint brush comb, which has metal teeth, to straighten elements and get rid of excess oil. Stroke the bristling from the ferrule to the tips.

By the way, do *not* pre-condition a brush in linseed oil if you are going to use it in lacquer or shellac immediately.

9

Photo shows that to avoid lap marks you should paint from dry into painted areas.

Using brush with bristles turned edge-wise ruins it by forcing elements out of shape.

Dip brush half-way into paint and tap off excess. Don't draw filaments on can's lip.

The linseed oil, which is not compatible with lacquer and shellac, will cause thinning of these products. This will lead to a dull or cloudy finish.

Before painting with a new nylon paint brush, wash it in soap and water. Comb it with a paint brush comb. When clean, dip the brush into paint halfway to the ferrule. Then, tap it lightly five or six times against the side of the paint container.

USING YOUR PAINT BRUSH

There are several important tips you will want to keep in mind when using a paint brush to help you get the best possible job and help you to avoid brush failure. These are as follows:

● Hold the brush in a way that is most comfortable for you.

● Use long, steady strokes. Do not bear down hard. Let the brush do the work. As you finish each stroke, lift the brush slightly to feather the edge.

● Always start to paint at the top of a wall and work toward the bottom. Paint a strip that is two to three feet wide. Then, finish the strip before starting the next one. This prevents paint from drying at the edges before fresh paint is applied, which will leave lap marks.

● Apply paint from dry into freshly painted areas. This blending of the paint prevents lap marks.

● After applying a few brushfuls of paint, run the tips of your unloaded brush lightly over the wet paint to smooth it.

● Every so often, slap both sides of the brush against an unpainted area to release any paint that has accumulated in the heel.

● Never paint with elements turned sideways. This will cause the brush to curl. Keep elements flat against the surface.

● The proper way to dip a brush into paint is to first pour paint from the paint can into a clean, rimless container. Fill the container halfway. Dip elements halfway into the paint to keep paint from getting into the heel of the brush. Tap the brush lightly against the side of the container two or three times to release

Always use right brush for job. Above, the bristles of brush are being forced apart.

excess paint. Never draw the brush across the lip of the container. This causes the brush to finger—that is, elements will clump and part.

● Never use your brush to stir paint. This causes elements to become soft and floppy. Use a mixing paddle.

● If you stop painting for a short while, do not toss the brush into the paint container, so elements rest on the bottom. Instead lay the brush flat on a flat surface. However, if you are painting with a water-emulsion paint, wrap the brush in a damp cloth to keep elements soft and pliable. This type of paint dries quickly and can stiffen the elements.

PROPER CLEANING

Always clean your brush immediately after using it.

Cleaning a brush properly assures that it will be ready for use next time you need it. The important thing to remember is that the cleaner you use is the same solvent which is used to thin the paint.

Specifically, use turpentine or mineral spirits to clean a brush that has been used in an oil-base paint, enamel, or varnish. Use alcohol as your cleaning agent if the brush was used in shellac, and use lacquer thinner for a brush used in lacquer. To clean a brush that has been used to apply a water-emulsion paint, use soap and water.

Let the brush soak in the cleaner for several minutes. Then, work the elements against the side of the cleaning container to loosen and draw off paint. Squeeze the elements from heel to the tips of the brush to work out all paint. If paint is caked on the brush, scrape it with a putty knife. Keep repeating the cleaning operation until the brush is clean.

If you are going to store the brush, wash it with a mild soap and warm water after cleaning. Shake out excess and comb the bristles with a brush comb to straighten them. Let the brush dry by suspending it by the handle from a hook.

11

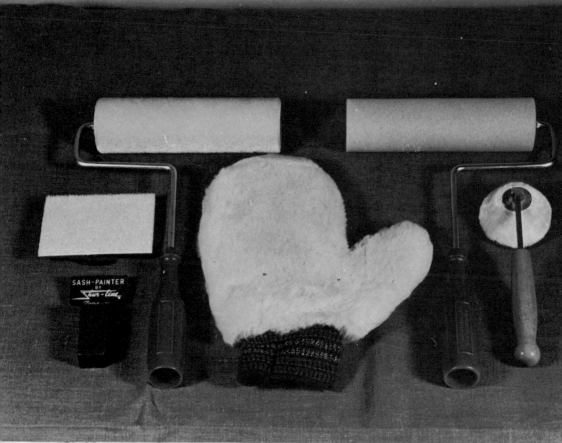

In the "roller" catagory, photo shows two 7-in. rollers, one mohair, the other a dynel-nylon blend. Glove is a painter's mitt, small roller is for painting corners, small rectangle is for baseboards and along wall tops. Small tool is a sash painter for windows.

PAINT ROLLERS

For the best results, select a quality roller of the right type

There is practically no area of the home that cannot be painted with a paint roller. This includes interior walls and ceilings, the entire outside surface of the house, trim and sash, pipes and other irregularly shaped accoutrements, floors, masonry, and even fences.

As with paint brushes, you get a professional paint job by selecting a high quality roller of the proper type. Time is the big advantage you gain in using a roller. Painting with a roller is faster than with a brush. However, you do not have as much control over a roller as you do with a brush.

SELECTING THE ROLLER TYPE

For painting large, flat surfaces (walls, ceilings, and floors), there are several types of rollers of different materials and nap lengths that can be used. Which type and nap thickness you select depends on the type of surface being painted and the type of paint being used. In addition, there are special rollers for special jobs.

The accompanying chart will make it easier for you to select the proper roller when painting large, flat surfaces inside and outside the home. It lists the type of surface which is being painted, the type

Paint or Coating	Smooth Surface	Semi-rough Surface	Rough Surface	Extra-rough Surface
Exterior wood finishes:				
Oil & alkyd paint	LS-¾″	LS-1″	LS-1¼″	
Latex house paint	DN-¾″	DN-1″	DN-1¼″	
Oil stains	LS-½″	LS-¾″	LS-1″	
Wood preservatives	LS-½″	LS-¾″	LS-1″	
Interior finishes:				
Oil and alkyd paint	LS-⅜″	LS-½″	LS-¾″	
Latex	DN-⅜″	DN-½″	DN-¾″	
Masonry paints:				LS-1¼″
Alkyd		LS-¾″	LS-1″	DN-1¼″
Latex		DN-¾″	DN-1″	
Varnishes	M-¼″			
Floor coatings:				
Alkyd	9″, 12″, 18″ M-¼″	9″, 12″, 18″ LS-½″		
Epoxy	9″, 12″, 18″ M-¼″	9″, 12″, 18″ LS-½″		
Latex	9″, 12″, 18″ M-¼″	9″, 12″, 18″ DN-½″		
Urethane	9″, 12″, 18″ M-¼″	9″, 12″, 18″ LS-½″		

Note: If using a primer, use the same roller that you will use for the finish coat.

Definition of Surfaces:
Smooth—smooth wallboard, putty coat plaster, sanded wood
Semi-rough—sand finished plaster or drywall, poured concrete, clapboard
Rough—textured plaster, light stucco, wood shakes, filled block
Extra Rough—Raw block, brick, heavy stucco

Key:
LS—Lambskin shearling
DN—Dynel-nylon
M—Mohair

of paint or coating material being used, which roller material to use, and recommended thicknessess of the roller nap. We will discuss special rollers following presentation of the chart.

TWO GENERAL RULES

Before getting to the chart, however, there are two general rules which should be mentioned. These are as follows:

1. Selection of the proper nap material is of primary importance. Generally, this material is of three types: a dynel-nylon blend, pure lambskin shearling, and mohair.

Dynel-nylon is a synthetic material which is recommended for use with water emulsion base paint, although you can also use it when painting with oil base paint. Lambskin shearling is a natural organic material that is used with oil base paint only. Never use it with a water emulsion coating. It will absorb water and be ruined. Mohair is a natural material with a short (1/4″) nap that provides the smoothest finish when applying enamel paint, semi-gloss paint, varnish, and lacquer to a smooth surface.

2. As you will note, in most cases on the chart the size of the roller is omitted. Where size is not stipulated, it should be understood that you should use a nine-inch roller. This is the size that most homeowner-painters can best handle without causing paint to spatter.

Where size *is* noted, more than one is given. The choice is yours. If, for example, you can control an 18 in. roller when applying a floor coating, by all means use this larger size. It will cut down on your work. Larger size rollers are easier to handle when painting or coating a horizontal surface like a floor.

SPECIALIZED ROLLERS

What about special rollers? The one you will have most need for is the trim roller for painting trim and sash. These run in size from one to three inches. Select the one size that coincides with the width of the trim piece.

The material of trim rollers is either of

13

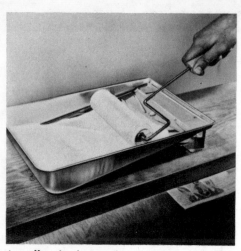

A roller is faster, but it pays, as when using a brush, to select a high grade tool.

Handy smaller trim rollers come in one to 3-inch widths for painting trim and sash.

dynel-nylon, lambskin shearling, or mohair. Use the chart to select the correct material for your needs.

You will also have need for a corner roller, which has a beveled donut-shape to allow painting in corners and along the ceiling border where larger sized rollers won't fit. Because of its shape, you can butt the roller right into the corner and roll on a coating of paint that is approximately four inches wide.

There are pipe and contour rollers for painting large and small pipes, respectively. Also available are painters' mit-

tens. This is a lambskin glove which you put on your hand, dip into paint, and run over the surface. It is ideal for painting pipes, grilles, radiators, and downspouts.

CHOOSING A FRAME

In selecting a conventional roller, you will have to buy a frame on which to place the roller. This is not necessary for special rollers, such as trim rollers, which come equipped with a frame.

The best frame to use is the so-called bird-cage, which is of wire construction.

Use dynel and nylon rollers with the water-based paints. Other rollers won't stand up.

This EZ Painter pad is large enough to do clapboard siding and other exterior jobs.

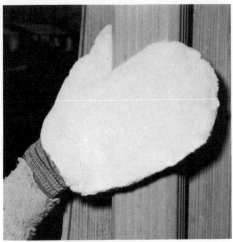

A painter's mitt is great for irregularly shaped surfaces. Your hand becomes a tool.

It is easier to clean than a solid frame and provides excellent rolling action. In addition, the roller sleeve is less apt to freeze to the frame as it might freeze to a solid frame, especially if you are using quick drying paint.

Another consideration is the handle of the frame. Make sure it is threaded to the frame and not held solidly. In painting surfaces which are out of reach, such as ceilings, you may want to use an extension pole. The pole screws directly on the roller's spindle when you unscrew the handle.

A sash painter is handy tool for painting narrow areas. Considered "roller" accessory.

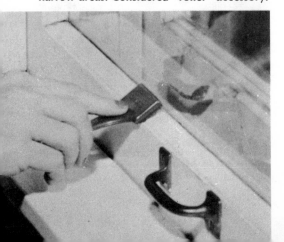

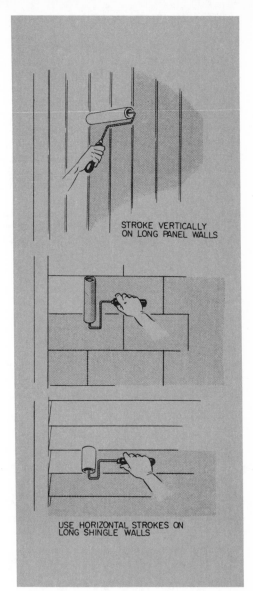

STROKE VERTICALLY ON LONG PANEL WALLS

USE HORIZONTAL STROKES ON LONG SHINGLE WALLS

THE PAINT TRAY

Another piece of equipment you will need when using a roller for painting is a paint tray. If the tray you select isn't equipped with a grid, buy one. This heavy metal perforated screen is placed in the top of the paint tray. After dipping the roller in the paint well, roll it over this grid to remove excess.

15

THE EXTENSION POLE

Finally, you may need an extension pole. These are made in varying sizes from two to 20 ft. long. It is strongly suggested that the pole you buy should not exceed 10 feet. Large poles are hard to handle and create the possibility of excessive paint spatter. Even professional painters avoid them, preferring to use a ladder and, if needed, a shorter pole.

Be sure an extension pole you buy is made of wood. Do not use poles made of

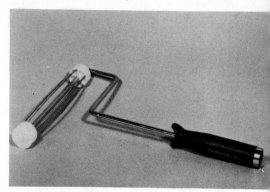

Bird-cage frame is best roller tool since it's easy to clean, has good roller action.

Extension poles extend your reach. These should be made of wood and not be too long.

Equip your tray with a grid to use for removing excess paint from your paint roller.

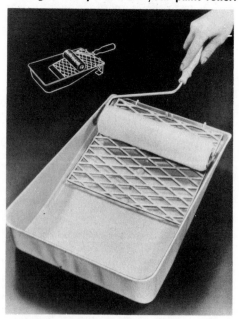

Clean roller in same thinner used in paint. Water based paint, here, cleans with water.

electric-conducting metal. They are a deadly hazard should they come in contact with a hot electric wire.

USING THE ROLLER INDOORS

In using a roller for painting the walls of a room, first roll on the border using a corner roller. Then, dip the conventional roller into the paint well, rolling it several times until it is uniformly coated on all sides. Roll out excess on the tray's grid.

Make your first stroke in an upward direction to minimize dripping. Start a short distance from the finished area and work towards it. After an area of about 2 ft. wide by 3 ft. deep has been coated with up and down strokes, roll the roller back and forth over the fresh paint while holding the roller horizontally.

Use slow, steady strokes until the roller starts to run dry. Then, dip the roller in paint again. Do not press down on the roller to get every drop of paint out of it. This can botch up the work.

USING THE ROLLER OUTDOORS

Using a roller to paint the outside of your house involves certain considerations. The way you prepare the surface for paint, for instance, is done no differently when using a roller than when using a brush (see chapters on "Preparing Exterior Surfaces.") However, chalking is a more critical factor with a roller and has to be handled more carefully.

When you use a brush, the bristles themselves disturb the chalky surface and lay the paint against the substrate for good adhesion. A roller, however, will not cut through chalk. Therefore, you should make sure the surface is as chalk free as possible before painting. Wire brush the siding and wash it clean with detergent and water. Then, rinse thoroughly.

The type of stroke you use when rolling paint on to exterior siding depends upon the type of siding. Use a horizontal roll to paint unserrated siding, such as clapboard, plain asbestos shingle, unser-

rated shake, and vertical plank. Vertical plank siding may also be rolled vertically if this is more comfortable for you.

With all serrated siding, such as cedar shake and serrated asbestos shingle, roll with the serrations (vertically) to assure that paint gets between them. The type of rolling action you use with masonry is of no consequence. Use any type of motion which is most comfortable, whether horizontal or vertical.

When painting exterior siding, make sure the roller is completely covered with paint, but not dripping. A roller which is dry in spots will produce holidays, which are areas that are not covered with paint.

In all probability, the fact that you use a fairly long-nap roller when painting exterior siding will make painting of the siding lips easier. The nap will generally extend up to the lips of clapboard and cedar shake, for instance, covering them with paint. However, keep a small trim roller or trim brush available to spread paint out across the lip should it start to drip.

Don't roll too fast. Use slow, smooth strokes. You won't avoid spatter, but you will minimize it. When working around shrubbery and walks, cover them with drop cloths.

CLEANING THE ROLLER

To clean a roller, first roll out excess paint on old newspapers until no more paint comes off. Slide the cover from the handle and wash it in the appropriate thinner or solvent. In other words, wash a roller used in a water emulsion paint in water. Use turpentine or mineral spirits to clean a roller used in an oil-base paint, enamel, or varnish. Wash a roller used in shellac with alcohol, and in lacquer with lacquer thinner.

Never wash a roller cover while it is on the frame. Paint will seep in between the core of the cover and barrel of the frame and harden, which could literally cement the two parts together.

After washing, allow the roller and other parts to air dry.

In addition to being fast and easy, spraying gives uniform coat, free of lap marks.

PAINT SPRAYERS

Once you learn how, spray painting can be four times faster

Although use of brush and/or roller is the more common method of home painting, many homeowner-painters have found that they can eliminate much of the drudgery involved in using these tools and do an excellent job with spraying equipment. A spray gun offers certain advantages which conventional paint applicators do not.

ADVANTAGES OF
SPRAY PAINTING

1. Spraying, if you are proficient at it, cuts the time of painting many times over again. For example, a four hour brush job can often be done in as little as one hour.

2. Spraying, if you are proficient at it, is easier. It eliminates the need for stooping, dipping, daubing, stroking, brushing out, and crisscrossing.

3. Spraying, if you are proficient at it, allows a more uniform paint job. The coating which is laid down is smoother, more even, and free of lap marks which often characterize use of a brush.

DISADVANTAGES OF
SPRAY PAINTING

Note the qualification, "if you are proficient at it." Unless you practice handling a spray gun before spraying on the finish work, you can literally make a mess of the job and of yourself. In addi-

18

tion, you must be able to make the proper equipment adjustments and be able to correctly thin out the paint. Another drawback to use of spray equipment is the initial outlay of money. An adequate compressor (1/3 horsepower is usually recommended for home painting chores), spray gun, nozzles, and necessary hoses will cost from $40 to $60.

SELECTING A SPRAY GUN

In purchasing a spray gun, there are various types of guns and nozzles from which to select. Generally, though, the type homeowner-painters will find most advantageous is a pressure-feed gun. With this type of gun, you can use both internal mix and external mix nozzles. By interchanging the two, you can employ most types of paints with your equipment.

An internal mix nozzle allows paint and air to be mixed together inside the nozzle. This setup is best for heavy-bodied paints and liquids. With an external mix nozzle, paint and air flow separately and are mixed just outside the gun. This nozzle is best suited for spraying of fast-drying paints, such as lacquers, water-base paints, and automotive finishes.

One thing to be certain of when buying a gun and compressor is that the CFM (cubic feet per minute) ratings of both are compatible. The CFM rating should be shown on each piece of equipment.

SELECTING THE PROPER PAINT

Another precaution before you paint is to make sure that paint consistency is correct for the gun. Brush-on paints right from the can are too thick for spraying and must be thinned before use. No general rule can be given here regarding paint thinning since there is such a great difference in the thicknesses of paints on the market. However, most paint manufacturers provide instructions. Con-

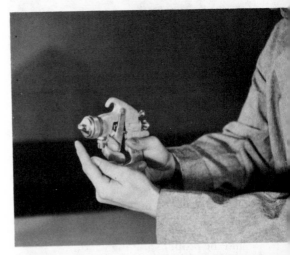

The DeVilbliss internal mix nozzle, above, mixes paint and air inside nozzle for the heavy bodied paints. Nozzle, below, mixes outside for use with fast-drying paints.

This small compressor and spray gun is adequate for homeowner who does small jobs.

DeVilbliss Co.

Thomas Industries, Inc.
Smaller spray equipment excellent for the painting of furniture, or even small rooms.

Big jobs require powerful compressors and large paint containers. You can rent them.

sult the label on the paint can or ask the paint dealer.

ADJUSTING YOUR SPRAY GUN

In using a spray gun, there are a number of adjustments which are extremely important. Results will depend upon the proper flow of material from the gun's nozzle, correct proportioning of atomizing air pressure with the flow of paint, and the proper spraying width.

Most spray guns are fitted with an adjusting screw which allows you to control the flow of paint from the nozzle. However, in practically all cases, it is recommended that this control be left in the wide open position and that the fluid flow be adjusted at the pressure feed tank. A spreader control affords a means of changing the spray pattern from a round spray to various width fan sprays.

Keep in mind that when making adjustments, an atomization which is too high will spread on paint that is thin in the center of the spray gun pattern. Conversely, insufficient air pressure will not

atomize the paint sufficiently and can produce a coarse, spattered effect. It is always necessary to spray scrap material beforehand for the purpose of checking adjustments by studying the spray pattern.

INCREASING GUN'S EFFECTIVENESS

Another reason for making tests is to enhance your efficiency in using the gun. Since the flow of paint from the gun determines the speed at which the gun must be moved across the surface, your speed of operation can often be greatly increased by using a setting that results in a fast flow. A comfortable, rapid stroke is best, because it provides sufficient paint coverage without runs and sags.

An important element to enhance efficiency of spraying is to keep a continuity of motion from the time you trigger the gun until the gun is triggered off and the surface is completely painted. This does not necessarily mean that the entire surface should be painted without

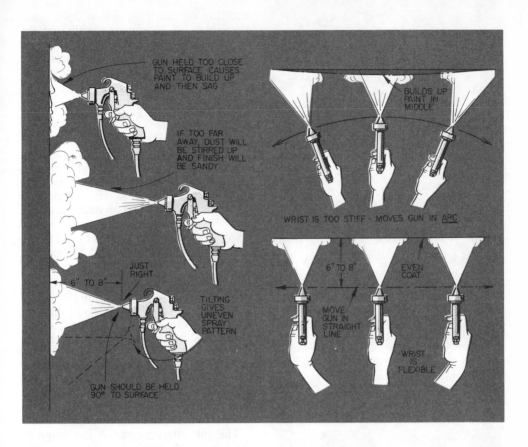

GUN HELD TOO CLOSE TO SURFACE CAUSES PAINT TO BUILD UP AND THEN SAG

IF TOO FAR AWAY, DUST WILL BE STIRRED UP AND FINISH WILL BE SANDY

JUST RIGHT

6" TO 8"

TILTING GIVES UNEVEN SPRAY PATTERN

GUN SHOULD BE HELD 90° TO SURFACE

BUILDS UP PAINT IN MIDDLE

WRIST IS TOO STIFF - MOVES GUN IN ARC

6" TO 8"

EVEN COAT

MOVE GUN IN STRAIGHT LINE

WRIST IS FLEXIBLE

Most spray guns are equipped with adjusting screws that controls flow and spread.
DeVilbliss Co.

To spray the outside of your house, cover bushes, etc., and wait for a windless day.
National Lead Co.

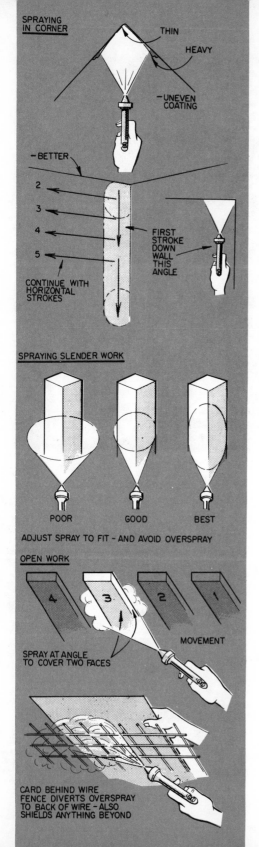

SPRAYING IN CORNER

THIN

HEAVY

—UNEVEN COATING

—BETTER

2
3
4
5

FIRST STROKE DOWN WALL THIS ANGLE

CONTINUE WITH HORIZONTAL STROKES

SPRAYING SLENDER WORK

POOR   GOOD   BEST

ADJUST SPRAY TO FIT - AND AVOID OVERSPRAY

OPEN WORK

4   3   2   1

MOVEMENT

SPRAY AT ANGLE TO COVER TWO FACES

CARD BEHIND WIRE FENCE DIVERTS OVERSPRAY TO BACK OF WIRE - ALSO SHIELDS ANYTHING BEYOND

shutting off the gun. But it does mean that this should be done wherever the shape of the surface permits.

The following discusses the important factors involved in spraying various types of surfaces around the home:

SPRAYING FLAT SURFACES

In spraying flat surfaces — walls and ceilings, for example — the gun should be moved parallel to and at a right angle to the surface. Keep the gun six to eight inches from the work. If you are too close, the paint will go on heavy and will tend to sag. If the gun is held too far away, there will be excessive creation of dust that can lead to a sandy rather than a smooth finish.

Use straight and uniform strokes, moving the gun backwards and forwards across the surface in such a way that the spray pattern overlaps the previous stroke by 50 percent. Never arc or tilt the gun although, as will be shown below, tilting might be necessary with certain types of surfaces. Arcing the stroke will result in an uneven coating, with more paint deposited in the center of the pattern than at the ends.

The gun's trigger controls the action of the gun. You should practice using the trigger until you can handle it properly. Keep in mind that the further back you draw the trigger, the greater will be the flow of paint. To avoid building up the paint at the ends of a stroke, begin the stroke, and then pull the trigger. Release the trigger before the stroke is completed.

The accompanying drawing shows the correct technique to use in spraying flat surfaces. Each stroke is "triggered". The stroke is started *off* the work, and the trigger is pulled when the gun is opposite the edge of the panel. The trigger is released at the other edge, but the stroke is continued for a few inches before reversing for the second stroke. Naturally, the big point to keep in mind is to hit the exact edge of the work, maintaining full coverage without overspraying.

In order to reduce overspraying, you can use a method called "banding." This

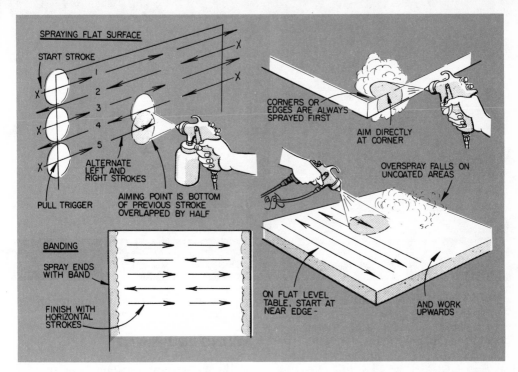

SPRAYING FLAT SURFACE

START STROKE

1
2
3
4
5

PULL TRIGGER

ALTERNATE
LEFT AND
RIGHT STROKES

AIMING POINT IS BOTTOM
OF PREVIOUS STROKE
OVERLAPPED BY HALF

BANDING

SPRAY ENDS
WITH BAND

FINISH WITH
HORIZONTAL
STROKES

CORNERS OR
EDGES ARE ALWAYS
SPRAYED FIRST

AIM DIRECTLY
AT CORNER

OVERSPRAY FALLS ON
UNCOATED AREAS

ON FLAT LEVEL
TABLE, START AT
NEAR EDGE -

AND WORK
UPWARDS

consists of painting on a vertical band at the ends of a panel. The vertical stroke is a single stroke that borders the panel and eliminates not only overspray, but the wasting of paint which occurs when trying to spray right up to a vertical edge with a horizontal stroke.

SPRAYING INSIDE CORNERS

If you spray an inside corner head-on, you will not get a uniform coating. However, the technique is fast and, if you are not too fussy, it is practical. When an even coating is necessary, each face of the corner is sprayed separately. This, in essence, is banding, as explained above. After making the vertical stroke at the corner, short horizontal strokes should be used to cover the area adjacent to the corner in order to avoid overspraying or double coating when you switch to your horizontal stroke.

SPRAYING EDGES AND OUTSIDE CORNERS

When a panel is to be sprayed on the edges and in painting outside corners of a wall, a modified banding technique is employed. One stroke along each edge coats the edge and bands the face of the surface at the same time.

SPRAYING A LEVEL SURFACE

When spraying a level surface, such as a tabletop, always start on the near side and work toward the far side. A certain amount of gun tilt is usually necessary for these types of surfaces, but when possible the work itself should be tilted up, so the spray gun can be held at as near a right angle to the surface as possible.

SPRAYING SLENDER WORK

The rule here is to make the spray pattern fit the job. Never use a wide horizontal pattern. A smaller horizontal pattern or a large vertical fan spray gives complete coverage without excessive overspray.

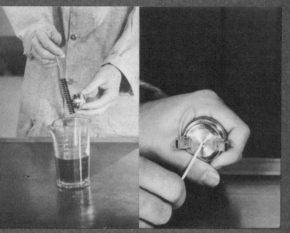
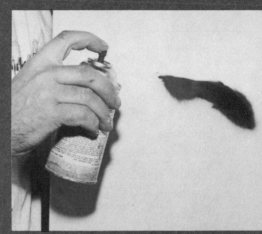

Be sure the spray head is clean. Wash it in thinner and then clean out the nozzle. Paint in aerosol spray cans is handy for small jobs, but technique still applies.

SPRAYING OPEN WORK

Iron grilles, fences, and similar work should be sprayed to get the most paint on the larges area with each stroke. A picket fence is sprayed with a single up-down stroke on each side. A wire fence and other intricate work should be approached at an acute angle. Use a shield, such as a sheet of cardboard, behind the surface to protect the area in back.

SPRAYING ROUND WORK

Cylindrical shapes, such as table leg turnings, are best sprayed with a round spray pattern and a vertical stroke. Use three or four lapping strokes to obtain full coverage.

Clean your spray gun every time after spraying and always at the end of the working day. Unscrew the cup, lower the suction tube into a container of suitable thinner, and spray for a few seconds until the jet is clear. Clean the suction tube, suction filter, and nozzle head with a brush dipped in thinner.

If for any reason you have not cleaned the gun after use and the pump has become clogged (the gun will fail to operate and make a low humming noise when you press the trigger), dismantle the pump, immerse all parts in suitable thin-ner, and clean with a brush until all encrusted paint has been removed.

OILING EQUIPMENT

If you are going to put the gun away for any length of time, oil the equipment as the manufacturer instructs in the literature which will accompany the equipment. If nothing else, you should spray a little spindle oil or light machine oil through the gun and put a few drops in the side of the housing (there is usually a lubrication hole supplied) to lubricate the motor.

AEROSOL CANS

Whether or not you want to try your hand at painting with professional type spraying equipment, you can still take advantage of spraying by using paint in aerosol cans. This innovation allows you to accomplish odd-and-end paint jobs around the home in a short time. Some of these jobs are painting of trellises, radiators, furniture, screens and cabinets.

However, there is a knack to using aerosol spray equipment. Keeping several points in mind will help to make your work easier and safer. For example, before you begin to spray, carefully read the instructions and precautions printed on the can's label. Immediately, you will

Painting picket fences is easy. Make sure spray pattern covers surface in one stroke.

notice that if not handled properly, that aerosol container can be dangerous since its contents are under extreme high pressure at all times.

Always keep the can away from heat, which can cause it to explode. The critical temperature is 120° but it would be wise to make sure that this amount of heat is never concentrated on the can.

Furthermore, since the contents are under pressure, never puncture the can. Never use this paint in a closed, confined area. Fumes are dangerous.

SPRAYING EDGES
AND OUTSIDE CORNERS

To begin the paint job, shake the can vigorously to mix pigment and vehicle. Shake the can often during the painting operation. You will hear a clicking sound every time you agitate the can. This is a marble which is placed inside the can as an agitator to assure full stirring of the paint.

As with professional painting equipment, it would be wise to try your hand at using the aerosol can before doing finish work. Paint a scrap surface to determine the best spray pattern. Use a back and forth stroke.

After painting, turn the can upside down and press the button until only pressure escapes. This clears the valve stem and spray head, and leaves the spray can ready for use next time you need it. Otherwise, the paint remaining in the nozzle will dry and clog the valve, which will render the aerosol can useless.

25

New paint is outdoor-tested at the National Lead Research Center in Hightstown, N.J.

HOUSE PAINTS

Those basic paints for exterior and interior main body areas

As used in this chapter, the term *house paint* refers to paint which is employed to protect and decorate the main body of a house, both inside and outside the structure. This definition is offered to distinguish house paint from special paints which are used for special jobs, such as painting of masonry and floors. Special paints are the subject of the next chapter.

When you consider the many different types of paint on the market today, you can appreciate why some sort of subdivision is necessary. There is a paint or coating for practically every type of surface and for solving practically every type of surface problem. Trying to tackle the subject of paint without some form of organization would be confusing.

DRAMATIC NEW CHANGES

Few home improvement products have undergone such dramatic and revolution-

	Oil-Base House Paint	Latex House Paint	Alkyd Enamel (Trim Paint)	Clear Finish
Wood siding, clapboard	X	X		
Wood siding, vertical	X	X		X
Wood shingles & shakes		X		X
Asbestos shingles		X		
Aluminum siding	X			
Plastic siding	X			
Wood windows & doors—screens and storms			X	
Trim, cornice, fascia			X	
Metal windows & doors	X		X	
Wood gutters	X	X	X	
Metal gutters	X		X	
Downspouts	X		X	

Closeup of panels shows that paint is tested on all types of siding, in all weather.

of flammable solvents. The primary type of high-gloss interior paint on the market at the time this was written was alkyd enamel, which has an oil base.

PAINT COSTS

Before getting into a discussion of the various types of house paints for interior and exterior use, there is one fact which should be offered. It concerns price, because money is a factor when you buy paint. It stands to reason that there must be a difference between two cans of paint of the same type when one is priced to sell for $5 or $6 more than the other.

Every manufacturer must pay practically the same for ingredients that go into paint, and each must make a profit or soon cease to remain in business. The obvious conclusion, therefore, is that less expensive paints don't possess the same quality ingredients or the same amount of ingredients as higher priced products. Lacking good or sufficient materials, the cheaper paint cannot provide good hiding power, durability, and wear-

ary changes in recent years as has paint. In fact, by the time you read this there will probably be even more startling paints available. For instance, manufacturers were in the process of developing a new high-gloss latex paint for interior use at the time this chapter was being prepared. This would be a water-thinned high-gloss paint which would offer the advantages of allowing clean up with water instead of messy turpentine or mineral spirits, little odor, and absence

In the laboratory, experimental pigments and coatings are prepared, then evaluated.

When finally tested, successful paints are put into production, cans filled as shown.

ability. In short, it will not last as long as a coating of good paint, and frequent repainting will be necessary.

On the other hand, you may encounter two cans of the same type of paint which have a price differential of only $1 or $2. In this case, the two could be fairly comparable in quality. The higher priced product is probably marketed by a nationally famous company, while the less expensive paint probably carries the label of a local firm whose costs of marketing are less. The choice, therefore, is yours.

INTERIOR HOUSE PAINTS

Interior house paints for walls, ceilings, and adjacent areas such as trim and cabinets can be categorized into four broad families: gloss and semi-gloss paints (considered as one), flat (non-gloss) paints, primers, and clear finishes.

Gloss and semi-gloss finishes are used primarily in kitchen and bathroom where spattering of the surface with grease, soap scum, and other hard-to-remove dirt is likely. Of course, there is no reason why you can't use either in other parts of the house if you prefer their appearance. These paints are washable and will withstand a great deal of scrubbing with household alkaline cleaners.

You will encounter three specific types of gloss and semi-gloss (also called eggshell) paints in a paint store: gloss and semi-gloss wall paint, gloss and semi-gloss enamel, and semi-gloss latex paint. You can ask for the one you want by these names:

1. Gloss and semi-gloss wall paints are the older types of interior paint with a gloss finish, but they are being superseded by gloss and semi-gloss enamels which offers additional advantages. However, you may still encounter some.

A gloss or semi-gloss wall paint contains an oleoresinous vehicle that consists of a resin and oil. Although easy to apply, the paint has the disadvantage of not keeping its gloss, yellowing, and not being able to withstand washing with alkaline household cleaners for an indefinite period.

INTERIOR HOUSE PAINT USAGE GUIDE

	Latex Flat	Alkyd Flat	Gloss Enamel (alkyd)	Semi-Gloss Enamel (alkyd)	Latex Semi-Gloss	Varnish
Gypsum board walls and ceilings (kitchens and bathrooms)			X	X	X	
Gypsum board walls and ceilings (bedrooms, living rooms, dining rooms)	X	X				
Plaster walls and ceilings (kitchen and bathrooms)			X	X	X	
Plaster walls and ceilings (bedrooms, living rooms, dining rooms)	X	X				
Basement walls, masonry	X					
Doors and windows, wood	X	X	X	X	X	X
Doors and windows, metal		X	X	X		
Baseboards and other woodwork	X	X	X	X	X	X
Wood paneling	X	X		X	X	X
Kitchen cabinets			X	X	X	X
Furniture and built-ins			X	X	X	X
Metal pipes and radiators		X		X		

2. Gloss and semi-gloss enamels are newer products. They contain an alkyd vehicle, which is a combination of a synthetic (alkyd) resin and oil. They retain their gloss extremely well, resist yellowing, and can be cleaned with an alkaline household cleaner for an indefinite period. Gloss and semi-gloss enamels also allow immediate washing after they dry. Drying time is a matter of an hour or two.

3. Semi-gloss latex paint is the newest of the gloss type finishes for interior use. The paint has a polymer base that is thinned with water and not with a solvent as is gloss and semi-gloss enamel. Thus, semi-gloss latex allows clean up of paint applicators and spatter marks with water. It has a mild odor, is not flammable, and offers all the advantages of gloss and semi-gloss enamels with the exception of immediate washing. This paint should be allowed to cure for about five days before you wash dirt marks from it.

There are certain precautions to observe when using semi-gloss latex. First, never thin the paint with turpentine, paint thinner, or mineral spirits. In fact, you should not thin the paint at all unless you use it with spraying equipment. Then, follow the manufacturer's instructions which are printed on the paint can label.

When you use semi-gloss latex to paint a surface that has a glossy enamel finish, the old finish must be sanded to permit maximum adhesion of the new coating. New surfaces, such as unfinished gypsum wallboard, must be primed before painting with semi-gloss latex.

Flat (non-gloss) finishes are used primarily in bedrooms, living rooms, and dining rooms where only superficial dirt on the surface is expected. Although minor smudges can be washed away with a damp sponge, these paints will fail if scrubbed or washed with an alkaline cleaner.

Normally, you would use the same flat paint for walls and ceilings. However, some manufacturers make a flat paint

Alkvd flat wall paint has good hiding power. One coat is usually all that's needed.

Many people prefer a low sheen on woodwork. An alkyd enamel with semi-gloss does it.

designed for ceilings only. They contain a greater amount of pigment than ordinary flat paint, which gives them greater hiding power, allowing badly soiled ceilings to be covered with one coat. Ceiling paints dry to a flatter finish than conventional flat paint and do not look well on walls.

Flat paint for interior use usually provides a smooth finish. However, there are flat paints that give textured and sand finishes. These are excellent for use on rough, marred surfaces although, if you like the effect, they can be employed on a wall or ceiling.

Textured paint is a heavy-bodied substance which creates a variety of effects. For instance, if applied with a roller, the paint dries to a heavy stipple; if applied with a brush, a striated effect can be created by brushing in straight lines; if you twist the handle of the brush back and forth, you will create a swirl effect.

Sand-finish paint dries to a sandy finish, which resembles concrete. The paint contains granules of perlite or a similar gritty substance. The paint can be applied with brush or roller, but if you use a roll-

er, work quickly to avoid lap marks. With a brush, apply the paint liberally, but do not brush it out to avoid creation of an uneven finish.

FLAT PAINTS AVAILABLE

There are two types of flat paint on the market: alkyd and latex. The following details the characteristics of each:

1. Alkyd flat wall paint has good hiding power. In fact, some alkyd wall paints are designated as "one coat" paints because of their superior hiding powers. If a surface is particularly dirty, you can usually avoid a two-coat job by using a one-coat alkyd.

Many brands of alkyd interior house paint (both flat and gloss) are now of the so-called odorless type. These are formulated with an odorless thinner which supposedly eliminates the drawback of painting an interior during cold weather with the windows closed. However, the National Paint, Varnish and Lacquer Association advises that you not take a chance. Make sure you have adequate ventilation when using any type of paint. So-called odorless paints, by the way,

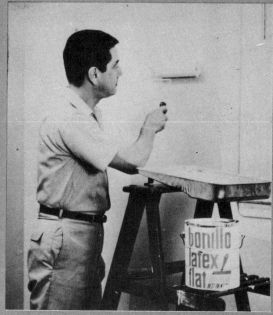

Semi-gloss latex is one of the newest on the market for interior use. It works well.

Latex flat wall paint offers the advantages of easy clean-up as well as good coverage.

give off odor as the paint dries and the vehicle oxidizes.

2. Latex flat wall paint has less odor than alkyd paint. Paint tools and spatter marks are washed away with water. However, clean up should be done before the paint dries. Once dry, it becomes a tougher job.

Latex flat wall paints are very easy to spread, but its ease of application can be a drawback if you are not careful. People have a tendency to spread the paint too thin, which will diminish the paint's hiding powers.

Latex flat paint should never be applied to a porous surface, such as unfinished gypsum wallboard, unless a primer is first used. The paint will fail to form a coherent film, which will prevent even minor washing without the film being rubbed off.

DRIPLESS LATEX

Many latex paints are of the so-called "no-drip" or "dripless" type. They have an artificially thickened consistency that makes them easier to handle than conventional latex and alkyd paints, which

are more liquid. However, the designation of dripless should not make you complacent. It would be dangerous to paint a room without first covering floors and furniture with drop cloths. If you spin a heavily loaded roller too fast, for example, globs of paint will be thrown off.

Dripless latex paint may end up costing you more money than an equal amount of conventional latex, because the heavy-bodied paint doesn't cover as much area

PRIMERS

Primers are used as base coats (undercoats) for finish paint. They are generally less expensive than finish paints and come in latex and alkyd form. It is not necessary to use a comparable primer and finish coat, such as latex primer and latex flat, although it is preferred.

If a two-coat paint job is required, you save money by using a primer as the first coat. Examples of when a primer should be employed are putting a light colored paint over a dark colored substrate, painting new material, and painting trim (window frames, baseboards,

31

Unlike the oil-base paints, latex allows you to apply paint to substrate that is damp.

Best results are obtained by applying a primer to bare wood areas before painting.

and doors) that presently has a varnish finish.

Clear finishes for interior use, at present, is a category of one: paneling and trim varnish. This product contains an oil or an alkyd base, with the latter being the better of the two since it has superior color retention qualities. Paneling and trim varnish is used on trim and wood paneling, providing the surface with a protective coating. Naturally, once varnish is applied, the true color of the wood is lost, but the grain is permitted to show through. A varnish coating darkens raw wood.

The accompanying table can be used as a guide in selecting paints for interior use. Where a choice of paints is offered, consider the characteristics of the products in relation as to what you want the paint to do. Where no choice is offered, the paint stipulated is the one you should use. For example, you will note that latex paint is not recommended for use on metal surfaces. Latex does not adhere to metal as well as an alkyd base paint.

EXTERIOR HOUSE PAINTS

Paints and coatings for the outside of your home fall into five basis categories: oil-base house paint, latex house paint, exterior alkyd enamel for painting trim, clear finishes, and exterior primers.

Oil-base and latex house paints are used for painting the main body of a house. Which one you should use depends on several factors, which are best summed up in list form.

Oil-base house paint offers you the following advantages:

● The finish of white oil-base house paint has a "controlled" chalking capability and will hold its "white" longer than a white latex finish. The chief reason for this is use of titanium dioxide pigment. The surface has the ability to self-clean itself since rain washes off the chalk and, with it, the dirt.

● Oil-base house paint provides a glossy finish if this is what you desire. In time, however, the gloss does dissipate.

● Oil-base house paint covers more area than an equal amount of latex paint and lays down a heavier film which has better hiding power. Thus, you can often get by with one coat of oil-base paint where two coats of latex paint may be needed.

● Oil-base house paint can be used to paint aluminum and plastic siding. Latex house paint has far poorer adhesive qualities in contact with these materials and should not be used.

Latex house paint offers the following advantages:

● Colored latex paint provides better color permanence than colored oil-base house paint.

● Latex house paint provides a matte finish if this is what you desire.

● Latex house paint dries faster than oil-base paint—hours as compared to several days. The danger of bugs and dirt settling on a latex surface, therefore, is lessened.

● You can apply latex house paint to a damp surface after a rain. The substrate must be absolutely dry before you can apply an oil-base house paint.

● Latex house paint is more resistant to blistering and peeling, because it provides a semi-permeable film which allows water vapor to escape.

● Since it provides a matte finish, latex house paint can be touched up without appearing "artificial". A glossy oil-base surface which has dulled with age will look touched up if a glossy oil-base paint is applied.

● Latex house paint can be applied to wood shingle. It is even better to use than flat oil-base house paint to control moisture. Flat oil-base house paint has long been recommended for shakes and shingles, but moisture escaping from beneath the shingles can cause a flat oil-base paint to blister. Not so with latex. When using latex over cedar or redwood, it is necessary to first use a primer made for these woods. This is to prevent water soluble extractives in the wood from "bleeding" into the paint, causing discoloration.

By the way, concerning the accompanying exterior paint chart, it indicates that latex is the best paint to use on shingles and shakes. This is true. However, shingles and shakes can also be finished with a preservative or stain, and they can be bleached. These techniques are discussed in the chapter on "Exterior Painting."

● Latex house paint provides easier clean up.

Neither oil-base nor latex house paints are recommended for a home's trim areas. Oil-base paint doesn't retain its gloss, and the matte finish of latex makes it unsuitable for trim.

Alkyd trim enamels are made with long-oil resins that have a high proportion of fatty acids. The paint brushes on easily and retains its gloss and color exceptionally well. Newer silicone-alkyd trim enamels are substantially more durable than conventional alkyd trim enamels.

Clear finishes are often preferred by homeowners who wish to retain the natural beauty of wood siding. However, no clear finish can be expected to approach the durability of a vehicle protected by a pigment (that is, paint).

At present, there is no clear finish on the market which doesn't have some undesirable characteristic. As a class, they are transparent to ultra-violet light (sunlight). The ultra-violet rays penetrate the clear finish and change the wood's surface, causing failure of the clear coating. Some clear coatings are fortified with an ultra-violet absorber and last somewhat longer than conventional type clear coatings. However, it is true for all clear coatings that success in their use depends on frequent re-coating of the exterior before failure occurs.

Primers for wood siding are of three general types: oil primers, a fortified primer of oil and a resin, and a latex primer. The first two should be used if the house is to be painted with an oil-base paint. Use a latex primer if a latex house paint is to be used as the finish coat.

Oil primers contain a bodied oil to control penetration into the wood. Fortified primers are similar to oil primers, but because of resins added to the vehicle, they are faster drying, resist bleeding, and resist mold and moisture. Latex vehicle primers contain some oil to help develop sufficient adeshion, particularly over old, chalky surfaces.

The accompanying chart can be used as a guide in selecting paints for exterior use.

Latex masonry paint provides excellent coverage of all types of masonry in the home.

SPECIAL PAINTS

A variety of masonry paints, catalyst coatings and varnishes

There are surfaces around the home which circumstances dictate should have a specially designed paint or coating. For example, the surface might be subjected to unusually heavy traffic as in the case of floors. Or it might be subjected to extraordinary moisture conditions that can cause a conventional paint to break down.

The purpose of this chapter is to acquaint you with those special paints and coatings for which you will have the greatest need. They include masonry paints and synthetic resin varnish coatings.

MASONRY PAINTS

Unless protected by a coating, raw masonry can eventually dust, scale, and crumble under attack by moisture and abrasion. There are five basic types of special masonry coatings from which to choose. Each is designed for a specific

Type of Paint	For What Job	Where to Use	Precautions
Portland cement paint	Sealing new or old unfinished masonry paint	Inside	• Dampen surface before application; keep new finish damp for 48-72 hours • Don't use on masonry floors
Latex masonry paint	Preserving new, but not raw previously finished masonry.	Inside and outside	• Don't use on new surface; allow aging • Don't use wall paint on floors • Don't apply to areas where water is prevalent • Treat previously finished surfaces with a conditioner • Prime metal that is close to the masonry surface
Floor and deck paint (oil-base, rubber-base or latex)	Finishing masonry floors	Inside and outside	• Don't use on vertical surfaces
Rubber-base swimming pool paint	Painting swimming pools	Inside and outside	• Don't use on floors • Can be used on masonry walls other than pools
Catalyst coatings	Strongest coating for tough problems	Inside and outside	• Expensive, so make sure you really need it • Must be mixed thoroughly • Short pot life

type of task. The coatings and the jobs they fulfill are as follows:

1. Portland cement paint is the oldest of the masonry coatings, but one of the best for sealing porous interior masonry walls which have not been painted before. It is inexpensive, alkali resistant, and resistant to penetration by moisture. If used out-of-doors, portland cement paint chalks freely. There are better coatings available for exterior use.

Portland cement paint has the ability to penetrate deep into and seal the surface of cinder block, rough poured concrete, rough brick, and porous stucco. It can be used over a surface previously coated with portland cement paint, but should not be used over a surface that possesses any other type of masonry paint. Neither should you use portland cement paint on a masonry floor. It will not withstand punishment.

Portland cement paint comes in dry powder form and is mixed with water as directed on the package. Before painting, the surface must be dampened. After painting, the surface must be kept damp until the coating matures. This takes from 48 to 72 hours.

As with any other type of masonry paint, portland cement paint should never be applied to a surface which shows signs of efflorescence, which is a white crystalline substance that forms as masonry loses water. Efflorescence can cause a paint finish to fail and must be removed before coating is done. Therefore, brush the surface with a 20 percent solution of muriatic acid. Allow the mixture to stay on the surface for four hours before flushing with clear water.

2. Latex masonry paint is designed for use on exterior and interior masonry surfaces which have been painted or are unpainted. Like all latex paints, this one is water-thinned.

Latex masonry paints are alkali-resistant and easy to spread. They have good color retention properties and good hiding powers. They prevent moisture from penetrating through masonry walls. At the same time, they remain sufficiently porous to allow moisture from within the wall to pass out and evaporate without blistering the paint film. However, keep in mind that latex masonry paint will not

Cinder block to right is unfinished, that on left is painted. Pores have been filled.

A 1″ or 1¼″ nap roller is good for painting masonry as it gets well into crevices.

withstand a steady concentration of water. Avoid using it where water stands or accumulates, such as in a swimming pool and below foundation level in contact with soil.

Before applying latex masonry paint, the surface must be dampened and absolutely free of peeling and chalking paint. These paints will not adhere to a chalky or peeling surface. Scrape the surface to remove peeled paint and treat the surface with a penetrating sealer or a masonry conditioner, which eliminates the effects of chalk.

Although latex masonry paint is alkali-resistant and will withstand chemicals emitted by concrete, you should not apply it to a freshly poured masonry surface. The amount of surface alkalinity present in fresh concrete could cause the paint to deteriorate. Allow fresh concrete to cure for a year before painting with latex.

Some latex masonry paints contain added chemicals that will allow them to withstand unusual abrasion, but not all latexes do. Before you use one as a floor paint, therefore, be sure it is labeled for floor use. If not, do not use it.

Metal stain marks are very difficult to remove from a surface painted with latex masonry paint. Thus, any metal

Stains that provide a natural wood finish are considered in special paint category.

objects in contact with the surface should be primed to avoid them from spreading rust stains on to the latex painted surface.

3. Oil base stucco and masonry paint has diminished in popularity since the introduction of latex masonry paint, because it is less resistant to alkali. Frankly, a latex or portland cement paint does a better job.

However, oil-base paints specifically designated for use as floor and deck enamels are still of use to the homeowner-painter. They contain resins to improve their resistance to alkali and have excellent abrasion-resistant qualities. They can be used with confidence.

4. Solvent-thinned rubber-base paints are of two types: floor and deck paint, and swimming pool paint. Each type is alkali-resistant, will not allow water to penetrate, and is resistant to abrasions. Generally, they are recommended for use in swimming pools, on walls exposed to water, and on masonry floors.

However, never use a floor type of solvent-thinned rubber-base paint on vertical walls, including those in a swimming pool. The additional pigment in this paint makes it heavy, and the paint will sag when applied to a vertical wall.

5. Catalyst coatings are of three kinds: epoxy, urethane, and polyester resin. They are the top masonry finishes on the market, but are also the most expensive. Two quarts of the coating, which is sufficient to cover only 100 square feet, cost about $12. Conversely, a gallon of one of the other masonry finishes cost from $4.50 to $6.50.

These coatings are excellent to use when an extraordinary problem exists, such as unusual abrasion conditions, when damage might result from moving appliances across a floor, or where chemicals, solvents, water or detergent are present in abundance. Otherwise, it would be a waste of money to employ a catalyst coating, since another type of finish would serve as well.

Catalyst coatings are usually two-part formulas, consisting of a base and a reactor which have to be mixed together thoroughly. They are available in colors and in a clear finish and can be applied to raw masonry. However, use caution when putting the finish over a previously painted surface. Many catalyst coatings contain strong solvents that can cause the old finish to "lift."

You can use a catalyst coating anywhere, but they do have a tendency to chalk when first exposed to weather. After initial chalking, however, the coat-

37

ing stabilizes and subsequent loss of film thickness is negligible.

If you decide that a catalyst coating is needed, you can save money by first applying a fill coat of a lower cost masonry product as an undercoat. Keep in mind that catalyst coatings have a limited pot life. Never mix more than you need. Furthermore, if you wish to take a break from work while applying the material, place the can in the refrigerator. The pot life of a catalyst coating is extended by lower temperatures.

There are one-part catalyst coatings on the market which come ready mixed with base and reactor. They have a longer pot life, but their performance cannot match that of the two-part systems.

The accompanying table presents a guide you can use to select a masonry paint for the job you are doing.

SYNTHETIC RESIN VARNISH

Development of synthetic resin varnishes have enabled homeowners to provide certain surfaces of the home with the most durable of finishes. A synthetic resin varnish is a mixture of a base varnish with a liquid plastic for use on floors, cabinets, countertops, furniture, and natural wood siding.

The coating that a good quality synthetic varnish provides is virtually like armor and withstands the severest knocks and abrasions, chemicals, oils, solvents, acids, boiling water, weather, and alcohol. Its protective and gloss retention qualities outlast that provided by a conventional varnish by three to five times longer.

Synthetic resin varnishes are of four types; depending upon the type of liquid plastic used: urethane, epoxy, vinyl, and amino resin. The one you should use depends on the job you are doing.

Urethanes are particularly recommended for use on porch floors and outdoor wood furniture. They can be used indoors if you choose, but the coating will eventually darken.

Before applying a urethane varnish, a coating of shellac or lacquer on the surface to be refinished must be removed in its entirety or the new coating can peel. This differs from application of other types of synthetic coatings, which require only sanding of a shellaced or lacquered surface. Furthermore, if a surface has an old finish of urethane, it must be sanded thoroughly to provide a firm base for the new urethane coating.

Epoxy has been discussed in this chapter under the heading of masonry paints. It is for use on masonry only and should not be used on wood. Uses and precautions as previously stated apply.

Vinyl and amino resin synthetic var-

Proper surface preparation prior to painting masonry is important. Remove all dirt.

Synthetic resin varnish is costly so only use where resistance to abrasion is needed.

Use of good quality porch and deck paint will brighten up entrance to your house.

Semi-gloss latex paint (special paint category) is good to paint ceramic tile with.

nishes are specifically designed for use indoors. Both are quick drying, provide good strength and resistance to marring, and are unaffected by ordinary household chemicals, cleaners, and solvents. They are recommended for wood floors, furniture, interior paneling, and trim.

Obtaining maximum results from each of the synthetic resin coatings demands careful preparation of the surface before application. Dirt, grease, wax, and other residue should be removed. This is best accomplished with a tac cloth.

If the finish you obtain after applying the first coating is too glossy for your taste, gloss can be reduced by rubbing with a No. 000 steel wool. This process should be repeated if a second coating is applied, but before the surface is waxed.

Two coatings of a synthetic varnish are recommended for raw wood. Unless a previous coating is badly rubbed off, one coating will suffice on previously finished surfaces.

Most synthetic varnishes are available in a clear finish and colors. They come in high gloss and semi-gloss.

Protect shrubs and walks with drop cloths before painting the outside of your home.

ADDITIONAL EQUIPMENT

Drop cloths, pails and paddles, all are as necessary as paint

In addition to brushes, paint rollers, spraying equipment, and paint, there are other items of equipment you will need to paint the inside or outside of your home. These tools and their proper use will be discussed as we detail the painting operation in the chapters which follow on painting the interior and exterior of the house.

However, the accompanying table of equipment is offered to allow you to get your inventory in order. The table tells you whether the equipment is needed for interior or exterior painting, or both.

USING LADDER WITH SAFETY

The remainder of this chapter is devoted to the use of one of these pieces of equipment (namely, the ladder), which if not employed properly can result in serious injury to the user. Perhaps the greatest pitfall the homeowner-painter must overcome in his use of the ladder is complacency. No one can afford a devil-may-care attitude while perched on the top of a ladder, whether he is five feet off the ground or twenty.

One of the most important steps in

A pot hook clamps onto ladder rung, holds can of paint at handy level for high work.

Piece of Equipment	Inside or Outside
Extension ladder, 12' to 28' depending upon the dimension of the house	Outside
Step ladder	Both
Drop cloths	Both
Caulking gun and caulk	Outside
Sandpaper, steel wool, wire brush, scrapers	Both
Cleaning cloths	Both
Hammer, nail set, putty knife, patching plaster, spackle	Inside
Mixing pails and paddles	Both

assuring safety is to inspect all equipment which will support you when you are off the ground. This is done by testing each rung by hand to assure that none is weak or has loosened. If it is possible to reinforce the weakened rung, do so. If not, don't take a chance. Replace the ladder.

Many painters extend planking to act as a scaffold between two step ladders. This allows them to reduce the amount of trips they must make up and down the latter while painting. A positive test is to extend the planking across two wooden boxes a few inches off the floor and bounce up and down on it to see if it is weak. It is also a good idea to nail brace pieces at each end and in the middle of the scaffolding for reinforcement.

The most dangerous part of house painting is when you are on a ladder. Falls from ladders kill approximately 1000 people each year and injure countless others. However, most accidents can be prevented by taking some simple precautionary measures to assure that the ladder doesn't slide or tip.

POSITION IS IMPORTANT

First, make sure you position a ladder

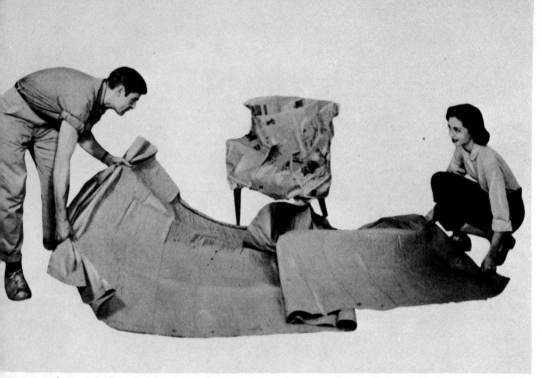

When painting inside, use plenty of newspapers, drop cloths, to protect everything.

Wire brush is one of the most useful tool in removal of loose paint, dirt and debris.

properly. Ladders should be placed out from the house to a distance that is equal to one-quarter of the ladder's overall height. For example, the bottom of a 24-foot extension ladder should be placed six feet from the wall.

The bottom of the ladder should be braced, especially if the ground is soft or the surface is of macadam. You can buy metal braces for the ladder, which are attached to the bottoms of the side rails. These are particularly useful to hold a ladder on macadam and also work well on soft ground. Or, you can drive a metal pipe into the ground which is firmly braced against the bottom rung of the ladder.

DO NOT OVER-REACH

One of the most serious violations of safety when on a ladder is over-reaching. Never stretch above you more than four feet. Never lean out away from the ladder. Your weight could cause the

Spreading a plank between two ladders will save you time when painting ceiling areas.

Sanding rough spots is best accomplished if sandpaper is attached to a sanding block.

ladder to creep, or you may lose your balance. Play it safe. Get off the ladder and move it.

Another dangerous practice is called the "push off." This is when someone on a ladder shoves the ladder away from the wall and shifts it in an attempt to change position. During the push off, you are momentarily floating in space, and the consequences just aren't worth the effort to save a couple of seconds.

OTHER IMPORTANT
SAFETY PRECAUTIONS

The following is a list of precautions to insure your complete safety when working at heights:

• Always wear rubber-soled shoes for the best traction.

• Never extend an extension ladder to its farthest limit.

• When lowering the extension part of an extension ladder, watch your fingers. Keep them away from the rungs.

• Never step on the top rest of a step ladder. You won't have firm footing and will have a tendency to rock.

• When ascending or descending a ladder, always face the ladder.

• Never employ metal ladders or wet wooden ladders when working near electrical wiring.

• Be careful when approaching gutters, chimneys and shingles for the first time. Look for evidence of wasps and hornets, and make sure they are eliminated before working on the ladder.

• If you suddenly feel nauseous, panicky or dizzy while on a ladder, it is probably due to nervousness of heights. Put your head through the rung and lower it slightly. Do not attempt to come down off the ladder until the sick feeling passes.

Before getting on a ladder, make sure it is firmly in place and won't slip or slide. Never over-reach on a ladder. If you can't comfortably reach, best to move the ladder.

PREPARING EXTERIOR SURFACES

Proper preparation of the surface is the real key to a good job

A paint job done with a good quality modern-day house paint should hold up for at least five years. The fact that many paint jobs fail sooner is usually not the fault of the paint, but of the painter who does not take the time to properly prepare the substrate (surface).

It is ironic that an individual who spends money for the best tools and the best paint will fail to take full advantage of the technological advances he has paid for by overlooking an obvious fact: painting a surface which is not suitable to take paint is a waste of time, money, and effort, because the paint will break down. You cannot get a good paint job by regarding paint as a cure-all and spreading it over a poor substrate. Even a substrate in the best condition needs some preparation.

THE BIG DIFFERENCE

According to the National Paint, Var-

Check window pane glazing. If crumbling, scrape out deteriorated putty, replinish.

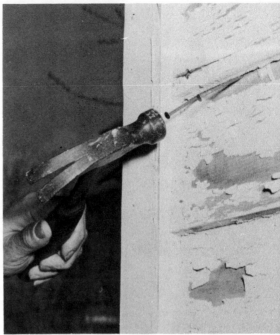

Split clapboard can be repaired by applying glue to crack, forcing pieces together.

To hold crack closed until the glue dries,
drive a few nails upward against the board.

nish and Lacquer Association, "We find
that 90 percent of the paint jobs applied
by the homeowner go bad long before
they should because of failure to inspect,
recognize and correct a paint problem,
and failure to properly prepare the surface. The big difference between a homeowner who undertakes painting and a
professional is a lack of patience on the
part of the former to take the time to find
a problem and correct it."

The best advice this book can give
is, "To take the time to find a problem
and correct it." The extra care you give
surface preparation now will result in
extending the life of your paint job by
several years.

Your first task is to determine the condition of the substrate. A poor substrate
makes itself known in one (or both) of
two ways: (1) The substrate itself is damaged; (2) The old paint surface shows
deterioration.

This chapter discusses damages that
are prevalent to the most common types
of siding which are usually painted. It

also explains how to repair two other
parts of the home which, if damaged,
could lead to failure of a paint job. These
are the roof and the drainage system
(gutters and downspouts).

The chapter following this one deals
with the question of why and how paint
fails, and tasks other than repairs which
are necessary to prep an exterior that is
going to be painted.

HOW TO REPAIR SIDING

Failure to repair damaged siding will
detract from the attractiveness of the
finished paint job and, more important,
will lead to failure of the new paint job.
For example, leaving a cracked piece of
clapboard in place and painting over it
will result in water seeping in through the
crack and getting behind the new paint
film, causing the film to blister and peel.

The following is a discussion of the
most common types of siding surfaces on
homes that usually are painted and how
to repair each prior to painting:

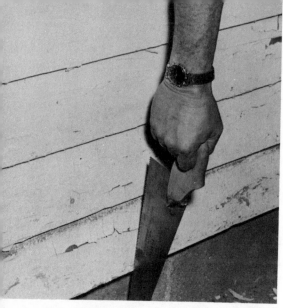

To replace rotted or damaged piece of clapboard, saw through on both sides of piece.

Carefully wedge out board above and free board by cutting nails with hacksaw blade.

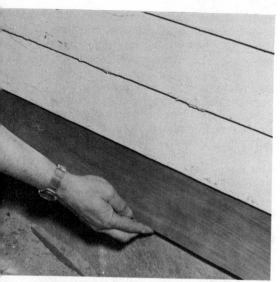

With bad piece of board removed, insert a new board and nail it firmly into place.

Caulk the new seam and sand down old board flush with new one. Caulking waterproofs.

CLAPBOARD SIDING

To repair a crack in clapboard, wedge the split carefully apart with a screwdriver and apply a liberal amount of weather-proof resorcinol glue. Do not apply too much pressure to the wedging tool, or you will break the board apart.

After applying glue, press the two parts of the split board together. Drive several finishing nails upward against the bottom of the split board to clamp the split together. Do not drive nails all the way in. Allow the glue to dry for 24 hours, at which time you should pull the clamping nails and plug the holes left by them with wood putty.

ROTTED BOARDS

If a strip of clapboard has rotted, you should replace it. Using a backsaw, score the board vertically about one-half inch from each side of the damaged area. Now, carefully chisel out the damaged piece.

Wedge out the board immediately above the damage area, and pull or cut the nails which were holding the bad piece. This allows you to remove the rest of the damaged piece you couldn't remove by chiseling.

If you accidentally cut the tarpaper beneath where the piece of bad siding was installed, patch it with black plastic roofing cement. Simply coat the damaged area with the cement and let dry.

Cut a piece of replacement clapboard to fit the area, slide it into place, and nail. Be sure to use galvanized or aluminum nails whenever you make any exterior siding repairs, since these are rustproof. Sink nails below the surface and seal all cracks and nail holes with wood putty.

Give raw clapboard siding a priming coat plus two finish coats when painting.

SHINGLE AND SHAKE SIDING

Nail split and warped pieces into place with aluminum or galvanized nails. If a shingle is badly damaged, replace it by splintering the bad shingle and pulling nails with a nail puller. Clean the area of wood splinters and insert another shingle of the same size and thickness. Give raw wood siding a priming coat and two finish coats when painting.

ALUMINUM SIDING

It is not difficult to restore aluminum siding which has been dented. However, be aware that repairs will be noticeable unless the entire side of the house is repainted. It is, therefore, best to wait in

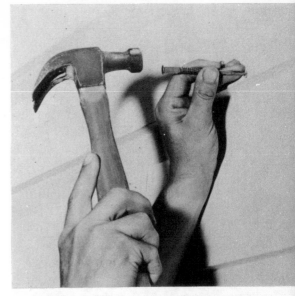

Prior to painting wood siding, set nail heads below surface, use wood filler; prime.

One way to avoid replacement of badly damaged sills is to coat with epoxy material.

After the epoxy is applied, lay fiberglass cloth over sill; apply more epoxy, then paint.

To replace damaged drip caps above windows, remove siding, cap, replace with new one.

making repairs to a time just prior to painting.

To repair a dented area, clean the area with trisodium phosphate. If dents are deeper than 1/16 inch, fill them with Sherwin-Williams Kem Weld, which is an epoxy type filler material. If dents are less than 1/16 inch deep, apply Sherwin-Williams Opex and Spot Putty.

Whichever repair material you use, allow the first coat to set for two hours. Apply a second layer and allow the patch to harden for 24 hours. Now, sand with wet #280 sandpaper, feathering the edges of the repair until they feel smooth. Wet-sanding is recommended, because it provides the smoothest results and keeps sandpaper from clogging. After sanding, wash the surface and allow it to dry for at least one hour before applying a primary coat of paint to the patched area. You can then proceed to paint the house.

ASBESTOS SIDING

Although it won't rot or weather like wood, asbestos siding is brittle and can crack or break if struck by a sharp blow. A broken piece of siding should be replaced to keep water from seeping in through cracks.

Break the damaged piece of siding into several small pieces with a hammer and remove as much as possible. Slip a hacksaw blade beneath nailheads and cut them if you can't pull nails with a nail puller. If necessary, cut a new shingle to size with a sharp gypsum wallboard knife. Score the shingle deeply and break off excess.

Slip the new shingle into place.

STUCCO

Fine cracks in stucco walls should be repaired before walls are painted to keep water from seeping into and widening cracks when the water freezes. To repair cracks, widen them with a masonry chisel. Wet the crack and apply a liberal amount of stucco cement with a putty knife. Feather the edges so they blend with the adjacent stucco.

Keep the new patch from drying too quickly, which will cause it to crumble and fall out, by wetting the area with a fine spray of water from a hose once each day for about a week. Once the patch cures, the wall can be painted.

HOW TO REPAIR A ROOF

Although it is not likely that a damaged roof will lead to failure of an exterior paint job, it will allow water to enter the house. This will completely destroy an interior paint job or wallpaper. Inspecting and repairing the roof can be done when you are preparing the exterior surface for paint.

Luckily, a home's roof seldom fails completely all at once. If damage is spotted early enough, you can easily repair it, preventing it from spreading which, eventually, will lead to a complete re-roofing job. This is expensive. Thus, no matter what type of roof you have on your house—composition shingle, slate, tile, wood, built-up—damage can be easily detected and fixed, as folfows:

COMPOSITION (ASPHALT) SHINGLED ROOF

These show damage in several ways. You may, for example, find small breaks or cracks in shingles. Don't neglect these, because they can enlarge to a point where replacement of the entire shingle is necessary.

Repair small breaks by applying a dab of black plastic roof cement in and around the break with a pointing trowel. The cement will bind the damage, making it leakproof. Excess cement that gets on adjacent shingles can be removed with a kerosene soaked rag.

Make sure the roof cement you use is a composition asphalt and asbestos type. This material expands and contracts with variations in temperature, and won't dry out and crack like ordinary roofing tar.

If a composition shingle has lifted away from the roof, apply a layer of

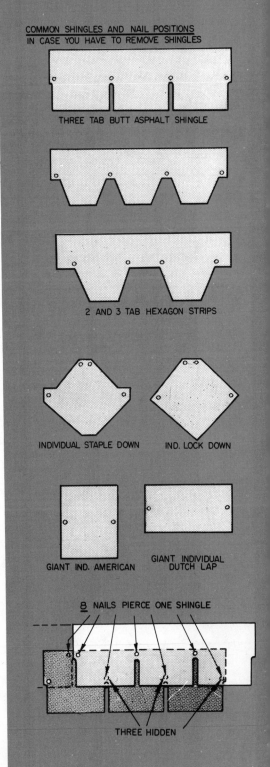

COMMON SHINGLES AND NAIL POSITIONS IN CASE YOU HAVE TO REMOVE SHINGLES

THREE TAB BUTT ASPHALT SHINGLE

2 AND 3 TAB HEXAGON STRIPS

INDIVIDUAL STAPLE DOWN   IND. LOCK DOWN

GIANT IND. AMERICAN   GIANT INDIVIDUAL DUTCH LAP

8 NAILS PIERCE ONE SHINGLE

THREE HIDDEN

Repair lifted roof shingle by "gluing" it back down with black plastic roof cement.

To remove bad composition shingle, remove all nails. See drawing showing eight nails.

After nails are removed, pull the shingle downward and it will readily slide free.

New shingle is inserted by lifting shingle above and pushing new one firmly in place.

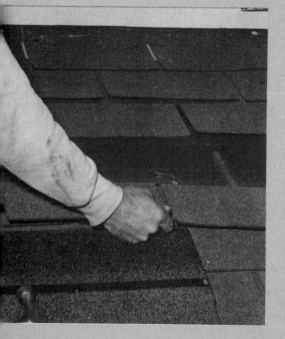

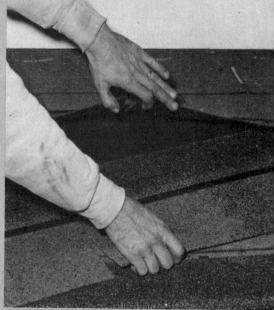

Breaks in flat roofs can be repaired with patches of asbestos felt and roofing cement.

black plastic roof cement beneath the shingle's edge and press it down.

DAMAGED SHINGLES

When you find a shingle that is badly damaged or is missing, it should be replaced. To replace a composition shingle, you must first be familiar with the configuration of the shingle your roof uses. This enables you to easily locate nails that have to be pulled before an old shingle can be removed. Common types of composition shingles and usual location of nails are depicted in accompanying drawing.

However, be aware of one very important fact. The nail locations shown are for these nails which are directly hammered into a shingle. For example, although drawing shows that three-tab square butt shingles are held by four nails, they are usually held by a total of eight. In addition to the four seen in the diagram, there are four others that are hammered through the shingle above and which extend into this shingle. To get at these "hidden" nails, you have

to lift the shingle two coarses above the damaged shingle. All nails must be pulled.

PULLING NAILS

Nails are pulled with a nail puller or claw. Carefully slip the damaged shingle from place after pulling nails. If the shingle binds, do not tug on it. You could rip the roofing paper beneath the shingle. Instead, examine the area carefully. You have failed to locate and remove every nail.

INSTALLING NEW SHINGLES

Install the new shingle by lifting the shingle in the course above and slipping the new one firmly into position. Make sure it is firmly seated. Fasten it into place with roofing nails, which are specially coated to prevent rust and stop leakage through nailholes. Roofing nails have large heads that keep water out of nail holes.

In inspecting a composition shingle roof, be sure to examine shingles that

Fix loose counter flashing without mortar by first cleaning loose mortar with brush.

Next apply a flash patching material with an asbestos-asphalt base that brushes on.

are over hips and along ridges. If a shingle over a hip or along a ridge develops a small break, apply a dab of black plastic roof cement as was explained above.

If a shingle over a hip or along a ridge is badly damaged or missing, it should be replaced. These shingles are usually held by only four nails. After pulling nails and removing the damaged shingle, use it as a guide to cut a replacement to size from a regular shingle. Make cuts with a clean, new razor blade so the shingle isn't shredded. Insert the new shingle into place and nail it down, but make sure that at least five inches of every hip or ridge shingle is exposed to allow water to run off.

TILE ROOF

Damage to this type of roof can be in the form of a slight crack, which requires a quick repair, or a bad crack, which requires replacement of the shingle.

Seal minor cracks with a coating of black plastic roof cement. Try to work the cement into the crack, but be careful not to spread the cement since the black material can mar the roof's appearance. Remove excess cement with kerosene.

REPLACING TILE SHINGLES

Replacement of a tile shingle is started by removing the two nails which hold it. There is one on each side of the shingle. Slip a nail puller beneath the nailhead and pull the nail out. Now, lift the shingle above the damaged one carefully and slip the old shingle from its position. You will need a leverage bar for lifting the shingle in the course above.

After the damaged shingle has been removed, lift the shingle above the area and slip the new shingle into place, pushing it up all the way to provide a firm seat. If the shingle you have just installed doesn't have pre-drilled nailholes, you will have to drill them yourself with a carbide-tipped bit. However, most tile

Save flashing around chimneys by reinforcing the area with asbestos saturated felt.

Asbestos saturated felt roof cement is also used to repair flashing on vent pipes.

Other natural cracks can be flashed with a patch of roof cement, asbestos felt strips.

Keep gutters in good shape by cleaning and carefully painting the troughs regularly.

shingles are pre-drilled. Nails used to hold a tile shingle in place are at least 1-3/4 inches in length to provide the strength required to accommodate the weight of the shingle.

SLATE ROOF

A slate shingled roof develops damage by cracking or shattering. If the crack is minor, seal it with black plastic roof cement. If the shingle is badly damaged, it will have to be replaced.

Two nails usually hold a slate shingle. They are positioned at the top of the shingle, beneath the shingle in the course above. The difficult part is to lift the shingle above without cracking it. Be careful. Now, slip a nail puller beneath nailheads and pull the nails. If you don't want to chance cracking a good shingle by lifting it to a point where a nail puller can be employed, then lift the broken shingle and slip a hacksaw blade under it. Cut off nails as close to the roof line as possible.

CUTTING SLATE SHINGLES

Cut a new shingle to size. When cutting, score each side deeply with a cold chisel. Hold the scored slate on a solid base and tap it slightly with a hammer. Finally, lay the slate flat so the score protrudes over an edge and exert downward pressure. Ragged edges can be removed by tapping with a hammer.

Slip the new shingle temporarily into place and mark off where nail holes are to be drilled. Place these holes as far toward the top of the shingle as possible. Make nail holes by hitting the marked-off spots with a center punch.

Before applying the shingle permanently, coat the area with plastic roof cement. Insert the shingle and complete the repair by driving home nails.

WOOD SHINGLE ROOF

The most serious damage that can occur to this type of roof is that shingles dry out. This can lead to dry rot. However, dry rot and other types of wood shingle damage — splitting and warping — can be prevented by coating the roof with a mixture of linseed oil and turpentine once every two years. This keeps the shingles moist and in good condition.

LOOSE SHINGLES

If a wood shingle has loosened, nail it firmly back into place. If you see a warped shingle, split the shingle down the center of the warp. Slip a piece of

To reinforce unpainted troughs so they will never rot, first clean with a wire brush.

Give trough a good vacuuming to make sure all particles and foreign matter are removed.

Reinforcement is done with fiberglass adhesive and fiberglass cloth like on boats.

roofing paper beneath the split, so it extends two inches to each side of the split. Nail down the split edges. If the outer edges of a wood shingle curl, they can be nailed down.

To replace a badly battered or missing wood shingle or one that has developed dry rot, remove nails with a nail puller. Wood shingles are normally held by two nails. Slip a new shingle which is of the same size as the old one into place and nail.

Incidentally, if a shingle is infested with dry rot, it should be replaced immediately. Dry rot spreads. Then, the entire roof should be coated with linseed oil and turpentine to keep the fungus from spreading.

BUILT-UP (FLAT) ROOF

Damages that can occur to this type of roof include curling and development of breaks in the top layer to reveal the sheathing beneath.

Carefully inspect edges where roofing material butts against a vertical section of the building. If roofing has curled back or has broken away, spread black plastic roof cement beneath the curled edge and press the material back into place. Insert a few roofing nails for added strength, and spread more roof cement along the entire edge.

PATCHING BREAKS

To patch breaks in built-up roofing, cut back the break with a sharp knife and remove all loose ends. Spread a layer of roof cement over the spot, extending the cement out about two inches beyond the area on all sides.

Cut a piece of asbestos saturated felt to size and lay it on top of the cement. The felt also should extend two inches beyond the edges of the damaged area. Press the felt into place and nail the edges down with roofing nails. Follow with a liberal application of roof cement around all edges.

To protect the patched area from the elements, spread gravel or dry sand over it. In fact, gravel or sand should be spread

If gutter has hole, apply liberal amount of roof cement and use aluminum foil patch.

Complete patch by coating entire area and foil with good quantity of roofing cement.

over the entire surface of a built-up roof.

FLASHING

Flashings are not roof shingles. However, they are an important part of roof construction and often require attention. These are metal strips, usually aluminum, that are used to block and turn water at those areas of the roof which aren't perfectly sealed surfaces.

Every roof has flashings. For instance, there is flashing around a chimney, in valleys, and around vent pipes. There are also flashing strips at intersections of roof and wall, and around dormers.

It is usually impossible to know for certain whether flashing which has pulled away from the roof is the cause of a leak. Flashing is usually applied beneath the shingles and can't be inspected without ripping out the roof. In the event of a leak, if you have ruled out such things as bad shingles, and clogged gutters and downspouts, then it pays to indiscriminately turn your attention to flashing.

HOW TO BEGIN

Begin by reinforcing flashing in those areas which experience has shown to be the most troublesome. One of these areas is the chimney. Flashing here has more tendency to weaken than anywhere else over the roof, because there is movement of the roof around the chimney as a home settles.

Examine the top edge of the counter flashing where it bends into the chimney mortar joint. Has it pulled away from the joint or is the mortar crumbling? If so, rake out and clean the joint to a depth of about 1 1/2 inches. Make sure the edge of the flashing is pushed well into the joint and remortar.

Now, examine the flashing at the corners of the chimney. If it has pulled apart slightly, an effective repair can be made by coating the joint with black plastic roof cement. If the gap is wide, cut a length of asbestos saturated felt or fiberglass duro-mesh to extend two inches around the corner. Apply a good amount of roof cement and press the material

Do not overlook doing as good a preparation job on outbuildings as you do on the house.

Check for areas you may have missed. Take down shutters and look for hidden joints.

into it. Follow by covering the felt or fiberglass with another coating of roof cement. The same procedure can be used to reinforce all corners.

CHECK VENT PIPES

Another critical flashing area is around vent pipes. Flashing often breaks away from the pipe itself. If the gap isn't too wide, the area can be sealed with an application of roof cement. To make an even more effective repair, cut a length of asbestos felt or fiberglass duro-mesh so it extends halfway up the pipe. Apply a liberal amount of roof cement up the pipe and press the material into place. Then, cover the patch with a good supply of roof cement.

REINFORCE VALLEYS

If flashing in a valley is suspect, there is an easier way to handle the problem than ripping up the roof. Simply reinforce the valley.

Spread roof cement down the entire length of the valley, extending it out two inches on each side. Cut asbestos felt or fiberglass duro-mesh to size and press it firmly into place along the valley. Cover the patch with a liberal application of roof cement. Flashing at other joints can be reinforced in the same manner.

HOW TO REPAIR A DRAINAGE SYSTEM

The purpose of a home's drainage system (gutters and downspouts) is to carry water away from the house in a quick and efficient manner. A clogged system can allow water to overflow the gutters and run down the side of the house where it can seep into cracks and get behind paint. Another consequence of a clogged drainage system is that water will settle around the foundation and could eventually penetrate through foundation cracks into the basement.

Wood gutters should be cleaned out once every year and coated with linseed oil or gutter paint once every two years. However, there is a way of reinforcing wood gutters to assure that they will never rot even though you may not main-

Entire house painted same color looks larger. Make sure bricks are ready for paint.

tain them periodically. This method can be used only if the trough has *never* before been treated with paint, linseed oil, or any other coating.

FIBERGLASSING WOOD GUTTERS

The method makes use of fiberglass cloth, which is available with fiberglass resin from marine supply dealers. The resin is used to adhere the cloth to the wooden trough, which forms a lining for the trough that will last for many years. It virtually assures that the gutter will not rot. The fiberglass cloth, by the way, is available in various size widths, and you can get a size that will fit your gutters almost perfectly.

However, success of the job depends on careful preparation of the gutter. Fiberglass will not adhere to a surface that is not clean. Therefore, all loose material, such as leaves and granules that fall into the trough from roof shingles, must be cleaned out. The trough should then be scraped clean with a wire brush, and all particles must be vacuumed away. If the inside of the trough is damp, wait for it to dry before applying fiberglass.

Now, coat the trough with the fiberglass resin and allow it to become tacky. Line the trough with the cloth and finally, brush on a final but liberal coating of the resin.

PATCHING HOLES

Suppose a gutter does spout a hole. You can repair it by first wire-brushing the area around the hole and cleaning away loose particles. Apply an even, heavy coating of plastic roof cement over and around the damaged area, and press in a piece of heavy household aluminum foil. Follow with another liberal coating of cement. This repair can be used for both wooden and galvanized steel gutters which have rotted in a spot.

Downspouts can clog up because of debris trapped in the pipe. This could cause water to back up into the gutter and overflow. Keep downspouts free by inserting a hose nozzle into the opening from the top (gutter-side) and allowing a forceful stream of water to run through the pipe.

59

AVOIDING EXTERIOR PAINT FAILURE

Diagnosing, curing and prevention of various deterioration ills

A paint surface on the outside of a home can fail for one of two reasons—

1. The home is damaged in some way or has a condition that causes paint to fail.

2. The paint was applied under conditions when paint should not be applied.

In any event, each type of deterioration denotes a cause, effect, and cure. The purpose of the discussion that follows is to enable you to recognize the types of paint failure you might encounter, what causes them, and how to correct (or prevent) them so they won't re-cur when new paint is applied.

Paint surfaces can deteriorate in several ways, as follows:

BLISTERING AND PEELING

This type of damage occurs primarily on wood siding. The cause of blistering is usually moisture which is trapped beneath the paint film and pushes the film up, producing "bubbles" which grow and grow and grow and finally burst. Paint peeling is an extension of blistering and occurs when blisters burst. The loosened paint film begins to peel away from the house.

Blistering and peeling can also occur if the paint was applied over a substrate that was too glossy, dirty or chalky. Occasionally, a dark colored paint will blister if paint was applied in direct sunlight on a hot day, causing the surface to dry before solvents in the paint evaporated. The trapped solvents can cause blistering.

The best way to determine if blistering and/or peeling is being caused by moisture is by the use of a moisture meter which you can borrow or rent from a paint dealer. Shove the meter's prods into the siding. The meter will record the

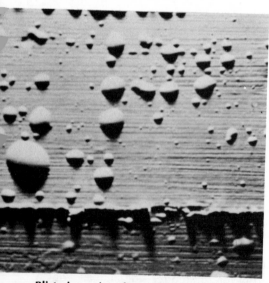

Blistering paint above shows harm moisture can do when it gets in back of paint film.

Never paint over blistered or peeled area. All loose paint must first be scraped away.

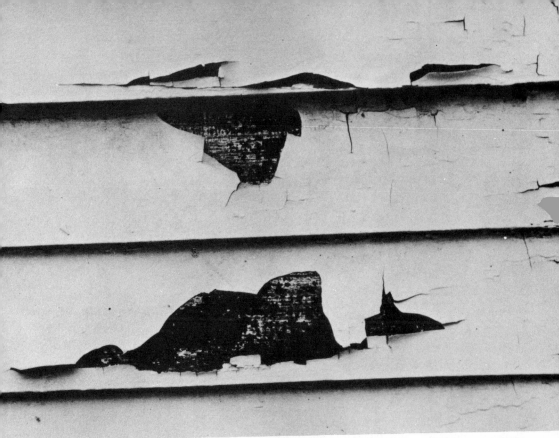

Paint peels when blisters burst. Sometimes paint has to be removed completely to wood.

moisture content present in the siding.

A reading of 12 or less is normal. If the reading is 13 to 20, you should not repaint with an oil-base house paint. However, you can safely use a water-thinned paint, which allows a certain amount of moisture to escape through its surface film. A reading of more than 20 means that you should not paint until the moisture problem is alleviated.

If blistering and peeling prevail because of moisture, the only way to assure that the problem doesn't recur after the new paint job is to eliminate, or at least control, the moisture condition. Moisture can be coming from inside or outside the home.

ARRESTING MOISTURE

To arrest a moisture problem, con-

sider the following:

● Check the basement or crawl space for evidence of dampness or condensation. There are several ways to prevent moisture from escaping from a damp basement. You can apply a vapor barrier over basement walls. This aluminum foil material prevents moisture from penetrating through walls to the paint surface. Or, you can install vent louvers through basement walls at ground level. Finally, you can place a de-humidification unit in the basement.

● To control moisture given off by the wet earth of a crawl space, cover the area with 55-pound roll roofing or a heavy polyethylene sheet.

● To cut down on moisture given off by home appliances, make sure automatic clothes dryers are vented to the outside. Make more use of kitchen, bath-

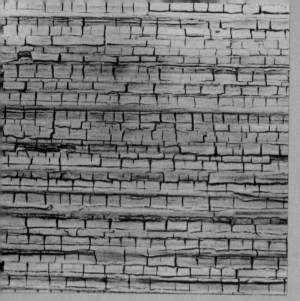

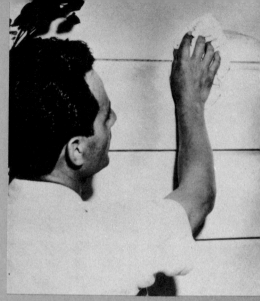

In the photograph above, we see paint that has developed a bad alligatoring condition.

Chalking gives home clean appearance for years. Wiped or washed, dirt is removed too.

room, and attic exhause fans. If these methods don't help, install de-humidifiers.

● Check attic louvers to make sure they are large enough to dissipate household moisture. A louver which has one square foot of open space for every 300 square feet of attic space is needed. There should be no less than two louvers in the attic — one on each end.

● Check shrubbery gardens around the foundation. If the earth is closer than six inches to the bottom course of siding, lower the grade line. Also trim shrubs which are growing against the siding.

● Make sure areas that require it are well sealed with caulking compound. A discussion of how and what to caulk is presented below.

After resolving the moisture condition, blistered and peeled old paint must be scraped off before new paint is applied. If the condition is bad and extensive, paint will have to be removed by burning and scraping. A propane torch is excellent to use for this operation. A more extensive discussion of how to get an old paint surface ready for painting follows.

EXCESSIVE CHALKING

Chalking is normal. Good quality paint wears gradually as it ages. The paint surface slowly gives off a powder that is washed away with rain. Washed away with the powder is dirt that has formed on the surface. Normal chalking of a paint surface, therefore, helps to maintain the cleanliness of the paint, and most paints are made to chalk.

Excessive chalking, however, is not normal. The paint film deteriorates rapidly. There are several reasons why this happens, as follows:

● It is possible that the previous paint job was not properly applied. The last coat of paint may have been spread on too thinly, or rain, fog or dew may have affected the paint before it dried.

● You may have applied the previous coat of paint over a surface that was too porous. Part of the paint's binder may have been absorbed rapidly by the wood, upsetting the paint's chemical balance and retarding its ability to chalk properly. To offset this possibility, make sure that the coating over which a fresh paint job is applied is not too old. A surface should not be permitted to chalk and wear off to a point that bare wood is showing. An old paint surface in good condition actually forms an undercoat for new paint. If this natural undercoating is worn away, it becomes necessary to prime the surface before a fresh finish coat is applied.

● A final reason for excessive chalking is that an inferior paint had been used. Poor quality paints are not chemically balanced to permit progressive, normal chalking.

HOW TO DETERMINE

How can you determine if chalking is excessive? Hold a double thickness of a coarse cloth, such as an old T-shirt, over your finger. Rub it over 8-to-10 inches of the surface. If this fills the pores of the cloth with chalk, chalking is excessive.

If an old paint surface is in good condition and shows only normal chalking, all you have to do prior to painting is to hose down the surface to remove dirt. If chalking is excessive, you should scrub the surface with a scrub brush and

cleaning solution. The solution consists of one quart of household bleach, one ounce of laundry detergent, three ounces of paint cleaner, and sufficient water to make 10 quarts of solution. After scrubbing the home with the solution which reduces chalk, hose the surface with fresh water and allow to dry.

Two coats of paint should be applied over a surface which has shown a tendency to chalk excessively. Two coats of paint should always be used if you put a colored paint over an old white paint. White paint is purposely made to chalk freer than other colors to maintain the white appearance.

If you are using an oil-base house paint, apply two coats of that paint. If you are painting with a water-emulsion paint, apply a suitable primer as the first coat to absorb chalk, and then apply the finish coat after the primer has dried.

GLOSSY SURFACES

This condition is the reverse of chalking. Shiny, glossy paint is found in protected areas, such as under overhangs, where weather can't get to it, and the

Never use paint that chalks near masonry surface. Chalk will run onto the masonry.

This is mildew. This condition will occur primarily in very warm and humid climates.

If paint you have isn't mildew-resistant, paint dealer can add mildewcide for you.

Paints containing mildewcide are mildew-resistant. It will say so on the label.

Never put even mildew-resistant paint over mildew. First kill fungus with a solution.

paint doesn't age by chalking. The surface remains very shiny and usually has a filmy coat of dirt over it. As you know, new paint will not adhere to a glossy surface, but will peel off in tissue-paper-thin strips. Therefore, before starting to paint

a surface of this sort, wash it with the cleaning solution mentioned above.

CHECKING AND ALLIGATORING

Checking is recognized by tiny cracks

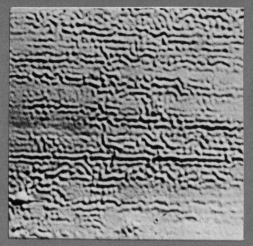

This picture shows how paint can wrinkle if you apply a coating that's too thick.

Unless paint has to be removed from a very large section, simply use a hand scraper.

which appear over the paint surface. Primary causes are use of a poor quality paint, or not allowing sufficient drying time between coats of paint. Checked paint should be scraped and sanded away before repainting.

Alligatoring is an advanced form of checking and gives the appearance of a sun-baked mud flat. It is caused by insufficient drying time between coats of paint, thinning the paint excessively, and applying paint over a greasy surface. Alligatored paint has to be removed before new paint can be applied.

CRACKING

Long, thin deep cracks that may extend down to bare wood, causing the paint film to curl at the edges, are caused by these factors: Excessive moisture on the surface when paint was applied; use of inferior paint, insufficient mixing of paint before application, and failure to properly brush out the paint when applying.

Cracked paint must be removed and bare wood exposed before repainting.

MILDEW

This condition, which is a fungus, oc-

curs primarily in warm and humid climates. Discoloration of paint by mildew can be avoided by using a paint that contains a mildewcide. These are made by most national paint manufacturers.

Mildew is characterized by splotchy spots over the paint surface. Where mildew has collected, wash it off with the following solution: 2/3 cup of trisodium phosphate, 1/3 cup of household detergent, one quart of household bleach, and sufficient warm water to make one gallon of solution.

WRINKLING

Wrinkling appears as a rough, wrinkled texture over the paint surface. It is often the result of applying too thick a coat of paint in an attempt to make one coat do the work of two. The paint surface dries before the underside, leaving soft paint beneath which starts to contract, causing wrinkling.

The condition can also occur if paint is applied to a cold surface. In this case, the sun dries the surface of the paint, but the underside remains soft.

Wrinkled paint must be removed and the substrate made smooth before repainting.

Before you paint, it's always good to first rinse as much dirt from siding as you can.

Where dirt is particularly stubborn, it may be necessary to first scrub with brush.

Latex caulk is easy to apply, quick drying, easy to clean, and makes an effective seal.

First beginning step to any caulking operation is scraping crack with a wire brush.

Remove small foreign particles and dirt by washing the whole area with turpentine.

Be sure to lay down a wide bead of caulk. It is impossible for you to use too much.

Unless things are totally out of hand, it is seldom necessary to remove old paint to bare wood over the entire breath of the house. In spots that are peeling or have alligatored, loose paint can be scraped away with a wide putty knife. If the damage is quite extensive, you may have to remove old paint from a wide area. In this case, use of a propane torch to loosen the paint before scraping will facilitate the job.

Usually, though, an old paint surface is simply faded, dirty and chalking. If not too dirty, the only preparatory step needed, other than caulking, is to dust the surface off with a brush. If the surface is appreciably dirty, it should be washed with household detergent and rinsed thoroughly with water. Allow the surface to dry thoroughly before applying paint.

When working at your home's windows, you can repair damaged mullions with putty.

RUST MARKS

Another thing that might have to be done is to remove rust marks from around nailheads with sandpaper or steel wool. Then, reset the nailhead below the surface and fill with putty before applying paint.

The one job that should be done before painting is caulking of seams and cracks. This is done although the old paint surface is in good condition. It is a precaution that will keep water from seeping beneath the paint surface, causing paint failure.

The most effective caulk now on the market for homes is latex caulk. You can, of course, use old-fashioned vegetable oil caulk. However, if latex is used keep in mind that it must be painted after it cures, or it will in time start to crumble. You can apply the same paint over the caulk as you use on the house, whether water-base (latex) or oil-base house paint.

STEPS TO FOLLOW IN CAULKING

1. If there is old caulking compound over the crack, scrape it away with a scraper and wire brush.

2. Wash the crack and surrounding area with turpentine or paint thinner to dissolve small particles of dirt and remove surface film. This cleaning will assure that the new caulk will firmly adhere to the surface.

3. Lay down a wide bead of caulk — at least 3/8 inch in width — making sure it covers the entire crack.

The obvious place that caulk should be applied is where window frames meet the side of the house. However, there are other spots, and these are generally overlooked. The following is a checklist to use to insure that all areas of your home which need caulking are caulked prior to painting.

CAULKING CHECK LIST

- __ Where chimney contacts roof shingles.
- __ Between dormer and roof shingles.
- __ Between siding and window drip caps.
- __ Between window sills and siding.
- __ Between siding and entrance overhang.
- __ Between siding and door frames.
- __ Between masonry steps, porches, patios and house foundation.
- __ Between underside of eaves and cable moulding.
- __ Between window frames and siding.
- __ Between siding and roof deck.
- __ At corners formed by siding.
- __ Between siding and vertical corner boards.

EXTERIOR PAINTING

Estimating the amounts and conditions, plus actual techniques

You are now almost ready to perform the easiest part of painting a house. Believe it or not, that part is the actual painting. Before discussing it, however, there are two questions that often bother the homeowner-painter:

- How much paint do I need?
- When is the best time to paint?

If you answer that first question wrong or guess at the answer, you will either run out of paint midway through the job or end up with more paint than you need. Such need not be the case if you employ the formula professional painters use to determine how much paint is needed to paint a house.

HOW TO ESTIMATE

The following is the step-by-step procedure to use for determining how much paint *you* need to paint *your* house:

Brush from side to side, completing section about 5 square feet before moving ladder.

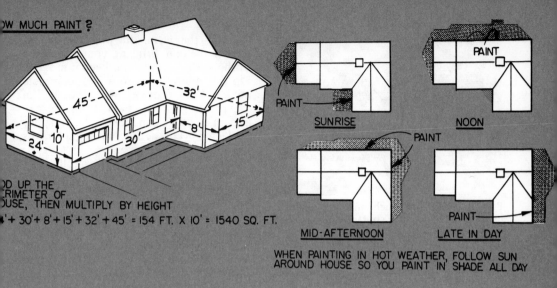

45' 32'

8' 15'

24' 10' 30'

)D UP THE
RIMETER OF
)USE, THEN MULTIPLY BY HEIGHT

' + 30' + 8' + 15' + 32' + 45' = 154 FT. X 10' = 1540 SQ. FT.

PAINT

SUNRISE

PAINT

NOON

PAINT

MID-AFTERNOON

PAINT

LATE IN DAY

WHEN PAINTING IN HOT WEATHER, FOLLOW SUN
AROUND HOUSE SO YOU PAINT IN SHADE ALL DAY

1. Determine the average height of your home. This is the distance from the foundation to the roof plus two feet for home and pitched roofs.

2. Multiply the average height by the distance around the foundation to get the surface area in square feet.

3. Determine how many gallons are needed by using the following formulas:

$$\frac{\text{Surface area}}{450} = \text{Number of gallons of primer required}$$

$$\frac{\text{Surface area}}{500} = \text{Number of gallons of finish paint required for each coat}$$

The figures of 450 (primer) and 500 (finish) are constants. Finish coats of house paint normally can be applied to about 500 square feet of surface per gallon. A gallon of primer will cover about 450 square feet.

The average height of my house, for instance, is 10 feet. It has a pitched roof, so I must add 2 extra feet, giving a total of 12 feet.

The distance around the foundation is approximately 300 feet. When I multiply the height times the distance, I find that the surface area of my home is 3600 square feet.

To determine how many gallons of finish house paint I would need I divide the surface area by 500. I find I need 7 gallons of paint.

WHEN TO PAINT

The best time to paint your house is when the weather is clear and dry and the temperature is above 40° F. Wait for morning dew to evaporate before starting. If it has been raining and the siding is wet, let it dry for a few days before applying paint.

If you paint in the summer when it is hot, you can assure the best results under the most comfortable conditions for you by following the sun around the house. By following the sun, you will be painting the shaded side of the house during peak periods of heat.

PREPAIRING AND PROTECTING

Two other tasks remain before you can apply the paint to the house: preparing the paint and protecting surrounding areas, such as shrubbery and walks. The latter is easily done by covering those areas which might receive paint spatter with drop cloths. As for preparing paint, it must be thoroughly mixed even though your paint dealer may have stirred the paint by mechanical means when he sold it to you. Mechanical stirring is not always thorough stirring.

The correct way to mix paint is to first stir it with a mixing paddle from the bot-

Boxing assures thorough mixing of paint — by pouring from one container to another.

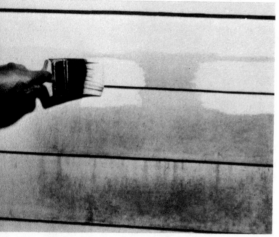

Make sure to paint edges of lap siding as, often forgotten, they are left unpainted.

"Feather" ends of each brush stroke for smoothness and minimal number of lap marks.

tom up — that is, mix the paint on the bottom of the can, bringing your paddle up to the surface while you keep it moving. Do this many times to assure complete mixing. Follow mixing with "boxing" of the paint. Pour the paint from the can into an empty, clean receptacle, and pour back again. This action thoroughly mixes paint vehicle and pigment.

Do not begin painting with a full can of paint. Empty half of a gallon into a clean receptacle. This allows you to dip the brush without drowning it. The brush should be dipped into paint only about two inches and then tapped against the side of the paint can to remove excess. Never pull the brush over the lip of the can, since this can damage the brush. Working with half gallon of paint at a time facilities proper brush dipping.

HOW TO PAINT

● Start painting from the highest point of the house, and paint from the top down. This prevents drips and spatters from spoiling previously painted areas. Start at gables and work down to eave lines. Paint dormers. If gutters are to be the same color as the main body of the house, paint them as you get to them. Other trim areas, such as windows, doors and accoutrements will be painted after the main body of the house since you will be using a trim paint on them. By the way, remove shutters, screens and storm sash before painting. These are easier to paint if removed from the house and laid on supports.

● Paint from side to side. It doesn't matter whether you work from the left or from the right. However, before you move or shorten the ladder, finish an entire area — about four or five square feet.

● Keep trips up and down the ladder to a minimum by taking all equipment that you can safely handle with you. Employ a strong, S-shaped hook to hold the paint bucket. Clip the hook to the ladder and attach the paint can to it. If you are using a roller, special trays are made that clip to rungs or to the side rail. These hold about three gallons of paint and have a grid which allows you to remove excess paint from the roller. Also available for painters who use a roller are short extension poles that are made to screw to the roller spindle. These allow you to extend your reach when on the ladder.

● Be generous with paint. Apply paint to the edges of lap siding first, and use a good covering amount. Then, brush out across the siding. Use smooth, even, back and forth strokes. Paint from dry areas into wet areas, and "feather" the ends of your brush strokes to assure smoothness and minimize lap marks where one painted area joins another. Don't bear down hard on the paint brush.

● If you encounter small holes in the siding, such as nail holes, slap the tip of a loaded brush smartly against them and then spread paint. This will tend to fill the holes, if not too large, with paint. Larger holes, of course, should be filled with wood putty before you paint.

● Once you have started to paint a course of siding, complete it before interrupting your work for any length of time. Otherwise, a lap mark will be created when you start painting again.

● If you are painting new work, a three-coat job is recommended—one coat of primer and two finish coats. If you are repainting a surface that is in good condition, one coat is often sufficient. However, if old paint is very thin or a long period between paint jobs has elasped, apply two coats of paint.

● If paint gets on glass while painting windows, place a soft cloth around the edge of a putty knife and wipe the smears away. This method permits a neat, close approach to painted putty lines.

PAINTING OF METAL

We have emphasized primarily the painting of wood and masonry. There are, however, many metal accoutrements on the outside of a home which need paint, including railings, outside lighting fixtures, mailboxes, window sash, gutters and downspouts, and even outdoor furniture.

Metal can be galvanized iron, steel,

To paint metal accountrements on house, use wire brush or sandpaper to remove all rust.

For best results, prime surface with either a red lead primer or zinc chromate primer.

You can spray or brush on finish coat of paint. If sprayed, protect adjacent areas.

Shingles, seen above, provide a relatively smooth surface. They are rived or sawed.

A shake looks hand split and has a rough face of vertical grooves, as shown above.

copper, aluminum, or iron. It all has one thing in common: each can start to rust or corrode if not adequately protected.

Rust and corrosion are caused by the chemical action of air and water on metal. All metals have a tendency to try and revert to their natural oxide state. With some, such as iron, this condition is a brown, scaling substance called rust. Iron oxide is rust. With other metals, such as aluminum, this reversion to a natural state produces a white powdery, pitting substance called corrosion.

There is but one way to prevent rust and corrosion. Air and water must be kept away from the natural metal. This is done with paint.

The most important fact to keep in mind when you go to paint metal is that the surface must be properly prepared to receive the primer and paint. Thus, as regards this point, painting metal and painting other materials, such as wood, do not differ. Preparation is of critical importance.

REMOVE RUST AND CORROSION

All rust and corrosion must be removed, even if this means scraping the surface down to bare metal. If you do go to bare metal, the need for an undercoating

primer before applying the finish coat becomes absolutely essential. Applying a finish coat of paint to bare metal, even so-called metal rust-inhibitive paint, and not applying a primer will lead shortly to more rusting and scaling, and destruction of the paint. There are, however, some paint products on the market which are advertised as one-coat application paints for metal. These can be used directly on metal, although two coats will probably be needed.

Now, if the present paint is intact and not rusting, you can wash down the item and use a soft-bristle brush to remove dirt. Then, if you wish to brighten up the metal accoutrement, paint it. However, keep in mind that if the item shows the least sign of paint failure, it must be scraped.

There's one more point to keep in mind. If a surface is partically rusted, it will usually require a complete paint job. Spotting leads to an unattractive result.

HOW TO PAINT METAL

● Wire brush and scrape or sand the surface with No. 360 wet sandpaper to remove loose rust and scale. Scrape and sand until all rust disappears, even if it means going to bare metal. Use plenty of

When finishing shingles, use vertical or horizontal stroke—whichever is comfortable.

When finishing shakes, use vertical stroke so finishing material gets into grooves.

pressure on the brushing and scraping tools. You can't hurt metal.

● Prime the surface. If you are not down to bare metal, use a red lead primer for the best results. If the surface is new or you had to scrape down to bare metal, use a zinc chromate primer. The difference is that red lead penetrates to the metal, driving air and moisture out. Zinc chromate prevents air and moisture from forming on bare metal. It forms the best undercoating for paint. Allow the primer to dry for at least 24 hours.

● Complete the job with a smooth coating of finish paint. You can use a regular outdoor house paint (oil base) for the finish coat or a rust-inhibitive paint. The outdoor house paint will provide a glossy surface, while the rust-inhibitive paint will provide a semi-gloss effect. Two coats of finish paint are recommended for maximum protection of the metal.

NEW METAL

New, bare metal surfaces require a somewhat different method. All new metal possesses an oily film that has to be removed. Wash it with mineral spirits, and allow it to dry. Then, etch the new metal to provide a good base for the paint, assuring that the paint will adhere and won't peel.

Surfaces other than aluminum are etched by washing with a solution of 1/2-pound copper sulphate to a gallon of water. Follow with a clear water rinse. If you wish to paint new aluminum, it is etched by roughing it up with steel wool. Be sure etched surfaces are absolutely dry before applying a primer.

If you live near salt water, you have a particular problem. Metal surfaces become contaminated by salt carried in the air. You therefore have to add another step to your painting procedure. Before applying primer, give the surface a good, thorough washing with hot water. This helps to dissipate the salt. Follow with a fresh water rinsing from a hose. Allow everything to dry, and then proceed to apply primer and paint as described above.

WOOD SHINGLES AND SHAKES

There is one form of wood siding which has to be selected here for special mention. Wood shingles and wood shakes are among the oldest siding materials. Yet, because of their roughened characteristics, they offer you a versatility not presented by other types of siding which

It is possible for you to finish shingles and shakes with good quality shingle stain.

As photo shows, you can finish shingles and shakes with good wood preservative.

You can also finish shingles and shakes by bleaching them out with a bleaching oil.

When painting shake siding, use a heavy hand to assure that paint gets in grooves.

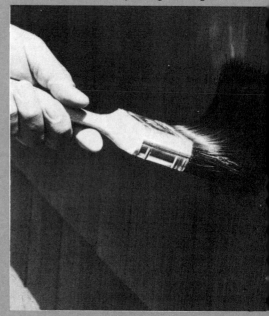

are smooth-finished, including clapboard, metal and even stucco.

Although wood shingles and shakes are handled much the same when you go to give them a finish coat, they are different. Shingles are sawed or rived thin and small, with one end usually tapered. In many cases, the face of a wood shingle is sanded to provide a smoother surface than a wood shake. This does not mean that the surface is as smooth as clapboard. It isn't. But it is smoother than the surface of a wood shake, and you can use either a vertical or horizontal brush stroke on shingles when finishing them.

Wood shakes, on the other hand, look hand-split, although they are, in reality, machined. Shakes are characterized by a rough face that has vertical grooves running the entire surface to provide a striated appearance. You can use only a vertical brush stroke on wood shakes when finishing them.

Another difference between shingles and shakes is that the latter is usually longer.

Modern wood shingles and shakes are primarily made from Thuja Plicata, which is western red cedar. This wood provides a pleasing color and grain for those who wish to apply a coating that will allow the grain to show through. It also has good resistance to decay.

FOUR METHODS POSSIBLE

There are four methods you can use to finish new, raw wood shingles and shakes. They are by staining, by painting, with a preservative, and by bleaching. The method you used or will use now if you are finishing them for the first time is dictated by the effect you wish to achieve.

STAINING WOOD SHINGLES

A good quality shingle and shake stain, for instance, contains, penetrating oil for preservative purposes and a small amount of pigment. It tends to colortone the siding, but allows much of the grain and texture of the wood to remain visi-

Special tool for applying a finish into coarse siding. Made by H&G Industries, Inc.

ble. Stains are available in a variety of wood tones that provide a flat finish.

PRESERVING WOOD SHINGLES

Preservatives penetrate deep into the wood, but leave little or no film on the surface. They are the most effective method of preventing rotting and decay. When first applied, the pigmentless, clear preservative allows the natural cedar finish of shingles and shakes to show through. However, because preservatives leave no surface film, they cannot prevent the wood from changing color. In time, then, the appearance of the cedar will change, tending to become darker. Furthermore, preservatives do not protect the wood siding against wear and abrasion.

All in all, a preservative is recommended in areas where a condition exists that can bring about wood rotting—for example, in areas near swamps and in heavy industrial zones. You can apply another type of finish to shingles and shakes used in these areas, but a more frequent maintenance schedule will have to be followed to provide maximum protection.

Pine knots bleeding through a builder's one-coat paint job. Sealing, painting is needed.

PAINTING WOOD SHINGLES

Shingles and shakes can be painted. Any good quality outdoor paint is suitable. However, painting shingles and shakes is a bit more difficult than painting smooth clapboard. Because the surface of the siding is rough, the thickness of the paint film applied over the wood's high points comes in for special consideration. Paint has to be applied with a heavy hand to make sure all the surface is covered and protected.

PRIME SHINGLES FIRST

Keep in mind that no paint should ever be applied to raw shingles and shakes. The wood must first be primed with a primer recommended by the manufacturer of the paint that you are using. Bare cedar has a tendency to "bleed" when it gets wet. The reddish-brown soluble substance will penetrate a single paint surface and ruin the job. Be sure to use a primer and two coats of finish paint over bare shakes and shingles.

BLEACHING WOOD SHINGLES

Bleaching of shingles and shakes with a shingle and shake bleach available from a local paint store gives a natural silvery gray appearance. This is the same as the appearance that can be seen on old shingled buildings which have been exposed to salt air for many years and are found along the Atlantic and Pacific coasts, especially in New England. The bleach speeds up the natural weathering process.

It is not recommended that you coat shingles and shakes with lacquer or varnish. These have a tendency to crack, leaving the wood exposed. When wood shingles and shakes are left exposed, they can turn black.

CHANGING THE FINISH

Now, what if you have shingles or shakes that have been previously finished, and you wish to change the finish? If the siding has been painted, there is not much you can do with it. The time, effort and problems encountered in trying to strip paint from shakes and shingles wouldn't be worth the result. In fact, it would be less expensive to reside the house with new shakes or shingles.

On the other hand, with a little effort, you can paint over stained, preserved or bleached cedar siding. The precautions are to use a primer recommended by the manufacturer of the paint you are using, and to use a latex or acrylic flat paint. Latex or acrylic flats are recommended because they allow underlying moisture to dissipate before it can bring the stain, preservative or bleach to the surface, which can ruin a paint job.

You can usually put stain over bleach, however, first place the stain on one shingle to make sure it gives you the effect you desire. When stain is applied over bleached wood, it changes the appearance of the wood.

As far as refinishing shingles and shakes, preparation of the surface is as important as when you paint any type of surface. All loose matter—dirt, dust, chalk—must be removed. A good washing of the surface prior to application of the finish material is always called for, as is a scrubbing with a wire brush if there is much foreign matter caked on the siding.

CEDAR SHINGLES "BLEED"

As we mentioned before, there is one characteristic of cedar which you have to contend with. This is the presence of water-soluble color extratives that could bleed out onto the surface and discolor the finish. This "bleeding" indicates that there is moisture in the wood. One way of trying to stop it is by taking the precautions cited in "Preparing Exterior Surfaces."

Despite all precautions, however, a small amount of bleeding can be expected during the first year after new, bare shakes or shingles are painted. It is recommended that you "wait out" this shakedown period. The bleeding will probably stop in time, and the spots that have appeared on the paint will either weather away or can be washed away with detergent and water.

When it comes to the actual application of the finish coating, it is strongly recommended that you apply it only with a brush, Unless you have experience applying paint, for instance, on a roughened shake or shingle with a roller or spray equipment, you can apply a coating that is too thin. This will cause the finish to fade long before it should, and may also lead to bleeding. Use a brush and apply a heavy coating of the finished product.

Use decking stains on outdoor wood. Clear finishes are a big problem, will not hold up.

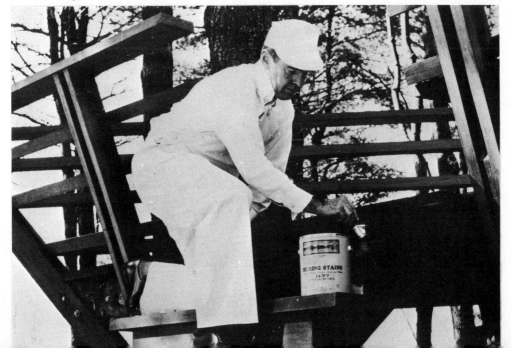

PREPARING AND PAINTING ROOMS

Check for any flaws and correct them before starting to paint

The complete paint job inside your home involves painting of ceilings and walls, painting woodwork, refinishing hardwood floors, and painting basement walls and floors. Each surface is prepared for painting in a different manner, and each surface is approached in a somewhat different way when it comes to application of the finish coat.

Naturally, painting of a room's walls and ceilings is the job most often done by the homeowner-painter. However, there is absolutely no reason why the same individual cannot refinish the hardwood floors in his home, or paint the concrete walls and ceilings of a basement if he wishes.

Material you will need to repair gypsum wallboard. Patching material is ready-mix.

To avoid confusion, since there is much material to be presented in regard to painting the inside of a home, the discussion is divided into two chapters. This chapter discusses preparation and painting of walls, ceilings and woodwork in the home's living quarters. The chapter that follows discusses preparation and finishing of wood floors, and preparation and painting of basement walls and floors.

Most of the homes in the U. S. now

Using roller to paint ceiling? Facilitate by clipping the roller tray to the ladder.

have walls and ceilings of gypsum wallboard, which is also called drywall and plasterboard. This material, which is usually four foot by eight foot panels that are nailed to the home's framing studs, is subjected to three types of damage that should be repaired before a fresh coat of paint is applied.

NAILS AND CRACKS

Nails that have been squeezed from the drywall panels and have raised the panels' surface is the most common damage. Drywall panels also have a tendency to develop cracks, particularly around window and door frames.

Nail popping and cracks are most often natural types of damages in that they result because of conditions prevalent in the home. A third form of damage — holes in the drywall — is caused by people.

However, no matter what type of dam-

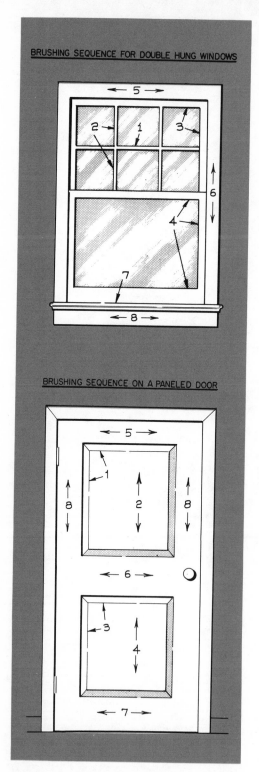

BRUSHING SEQUENCE FOR DOUBLE HUNG WINDOWS

BRUSHING SEQUENCE ON A PANELED DOOR

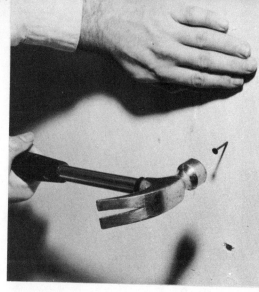

Nail that continues to pop can be stopped by reinforcing area with a drywall nail.

age you find on the walls and ceilings of your home prior to painting, if the repair is carefully performed, the result is usually permanent.

Nail popping occurs primarily as 2X4 wood studs holding the wallboard expand and contract alternately under varying humidity conditions. If your home is equipped with a forced hot air heating system, for example, less humidity is present in winter than in summer. Therefore, wood is drier and contracts during winter, and is more moist and expands during summer. This alternating condition forces nails holding the drywall up through the panel's paper-like surface, lifting that surface to leave scab-like circles. To effect a permanent repair, weak areas must be reinforced and patching material must be properly applied.

REINFORCE WITH NAILS

Start by reinforcing weak areas. Drive a 1 1/4 inch annular drywall nail into the panel and into the stud below. Position the new nail about 1 1/2 inches above or below the nail which has popped. Make sure the new nail is on line with the popped nail to assure that it penetrates the stud. As you drive the nail into place,

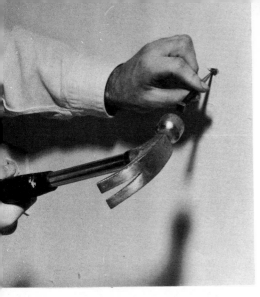 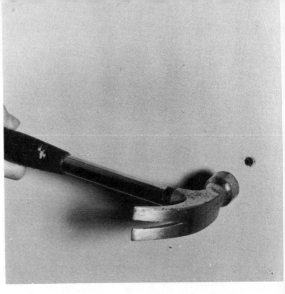

If nail is very stubborn and refuses to be reset by hammer alone, use nail set, as shown.

Popped nails should be reset below surface, wallboard should be dimpled for patching.

apply firm pressure with your free hand against the panel's surface to bring the panel into firm contact with the stud.

Hiding the nailhead is one of the most important aspects of the repair. Drive the nailhead below the panel's surface until the hammer forms a dimple in the paper-like material of the drywall. However, be careful not to strike the panel with a force that is too powerful. The drywall's plaster material will crumble and the nail's holding power will be reduced.

After the new nail is driven into place, drive the popped nail back below the surface. Again, make sure the surface is dimpled, but do not use your hammer too forcefully. If the popped nail protrudes out too far, refusing to be driven home, use a nailset to avoid the chance of damaging the wallboard with powerful hammer blows.

PATCHING MATERIAL

The reason for dimpling the surface of the wallboard is to give patching material a base on which to take hold. The patching material hides nailheads and, when painted, blends right in with the rest of the panel. The patching material

to use is spackle, which is available in powdered form and is mixed with water or in ready-mixed form.

Although ready-mixed spackle costs more—about $2 for a quart can—it is far easier to use than powdered spackle and leaves no room for error. If you use powdered spackle, it must be mixed to the proper consistency. If too loose, the material will run. If too thick, it will not adhere to the wallboard. Follow mixing instructions carefully if you use powdered spackle. These are given on the package.

Before patching, clear away loose plaster from around dimpled areas. One or two light swipes with a putty knife will take care of that. Now, smooth the area by lightly sanding with a fine grit sandpaper.

With a broad knife, fill each dimpled area full of spackle. Scrape off excess with your broad knife until the spackle is level with the surface of the wallboard.

Allow the patched area to cure overnight. Powdered spackle will shrink to form an indentation, and another application of spackle will probably be necessary before you can paint. Ready-mixed spackle does not shrink, so you can now proceed to paint. Before doing so, however, give patched areas a very light pass with a piece of fine grit sandpaper to smooth them out.

PATCHING CRACKS

Cracks in wallboard are caused by the house settling and shifting. Filling cracks with a patching material will not effect a permanent repair. A home's framework keeps shifting, and this movement will cause the patching material to eventually crumble and fall out. The crack will reappear.

The most effective way to seal a crack is by use of a fiberglass tape and a fiberglass adhesive or by use of ordinary drywall perforated tape and joint cement. The latter materials are less expensive than fiberglass. However, the fiberglass method is easier to employ.

HOW TO USE PERFORATED TAPE

1. Sand the area of the crack, making sure that you sand 6 inches to each side of the crack.

2. Apply a swath of joint cement over the crack and 1 1/2 inches to each side of it. Use a broad knife. Joint cement is available either in powdered or ready-mixed form, as is spackle. The advantages and disadvantages of each type were explained above.

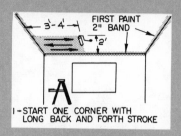

I - START ONE CORNER WITH LONG BACK AND FORTH STROKE

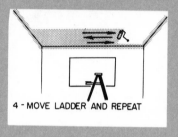

4 - MOVE LADDER AND REPEAT

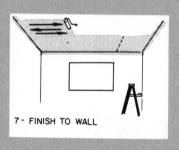

7 - FINISH TO WALL

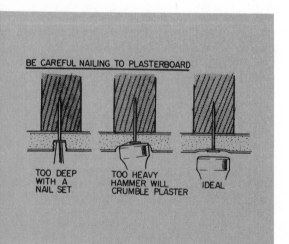

BE CAREFUL NAILING TO PLASTERBOARD

TOO DEEP WITH A NAIL SET

TOO HEAVY HAMMER WILL CRUMBLE PLASTER

IDEAL

3. Center a strip of perforated tape over the crack and press it down flat with a broad knife. Make sure the tape adheres to the wall firmly. Now, cover the tape with a coating of joint cement, bringing the cement out beyond the tape's edges. Remove excess cement and feather the edges so they are smooth and level with the wall. Allow the patch to dry overnight.

4. Apply another coating of joint cement to a point 1 1/2 inches beyond the edges of the last coat. Feather the edges, and allow the patch to dry for at least 8 hours.

5. Sand lightly and paint.

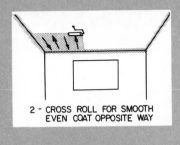

2 - CROSS ROLL FOR SMOOTH
EVEN COAT OPPOSITE WAY

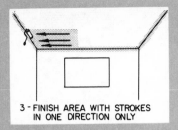

3 - FINISH AREA WITH STROKES
IN ONE DIRECTION ONLY

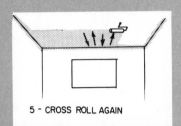

5 - CROSS ROLL AGAIN

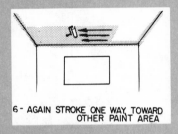

6 - AGAIN STROKE ONE WAY TOWARD
OTHER PAINT AREA

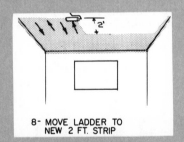

8 - MOVE LADDER TO
NEW 2 FT. STRIP

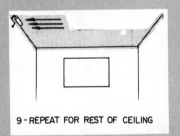

9 - REPEAT FOR REST OF CEILING

FIBERGLASS METHOD OF SEALING CRACKS

1. Sand the area of the crack, making sure that you sand 6 inches to each side of the crack.

2. Using a short-bristled paint brush, apply a generous amount of fiberglass adhesive to the area, extending the adhesive 2 1/2 inches to each side of the crack.

3. Press the fiberglass tape down over the crack and flatten it out with a window squeegee.

4. Allow the patch to dry until the adhesive loses its tackiness, which takes about two hours. Brush on a light coat of the fiberglass adhesive, feathering out the edges to make sure it blends smoothly with the wall.

5. Let the patch dry for 24 hours before painting. Sanding is not necessary.

PATCHING HOLES

Gaping holes in drywall can occur by accident or by design. For example, you may decide to remove an overhead lighting fixture. This will leave a whole in the ceiling that's about three inches in

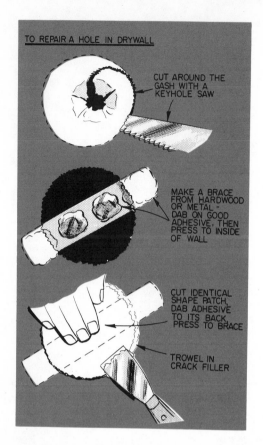

TO REPAIR A HOLE IN DRYWALL

CUT AROUND THE GASH WITH A KEYHOLE SAW

MAKE A BRACE FROM HARDWOOD OR METAL - DAB ON GOOD ADHESIVE, THEN PRESS TO INSIDE OF WALL

CUT IDENTICAL SHAPE PATCH, DAB ADHESIVE TO ITS BACK, PRESS TO BRACE

TROWEL IN CRACK FILLER

diameter. The best way to fill any hole of appreciable size in drywall is by making a plug from a scrap piece of drywall.

First, however, make sure the hole is large enough to allow you to manipulate the plug into position. The hole must be at least three inches in diameter. If it isn't, draw a circle around the hole to this size. Cut out the hole with a keyhole saw. Now, cut a circular plug from a scrap piece of drywall to a size which is about 1/8 inch smaller in diameter than the hole. Also cut a rectangular strip from the scrap drywall. Make this no less than two inches longer than the diameter of the hole.

For instance, if the hole is three inches in diameter, the rectangular piece should be five inches in length. This piece serves as a backing plate for the drywall plug.

Apply a liberal amount of joint or contact cement to each end of the support plate. Insert it into the hole and press it firmly against the back of the wall. Hold the strip in position until it takes hold. Then, allow it to set up firmly. Let it set overnight.

Now, coat the back of the drywall plug with a generous amount of joint or contact cement. Insert it into the hole and

After the nails have been reset, apply a liberal amount of spackle to dimpled area.

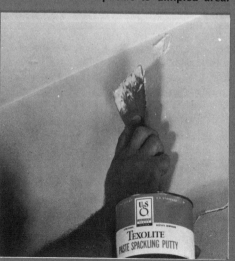

To permanently repair a crack in wallboard, you simply brush on a fiberglass adhesive.

gently press it against the backing plate. Allow this to set up for about 8 to 10 hours.

SPACKLE THE AREA

To finish the patch and get it ready for painting, apply spackle to the entire area, bringing the material out beyond the edges of the crack and feathering the edges so the patch is level with the surface of the drywall panel. Remove excess spackle, but make sure you fill the area full. Let the spackle dry. You might have to apply another application of spackle before you can sand the area until it's smooth and paint.

PLASTER WALLS

The second most common type of material used for the walls and ceilings of homes is plaster. With plaster, there is no problem with nail popping. Plaster doesn't use nails. Cracks do appear, however, but they can be repaired using the tape method as explained above. Larger cracks and damaged areas—those that are more than 1/4 inch wide—cannot be handled this way, though. They are repaired as follows:

REPAIRING CRACKS IN PLASTER

1. Chip away all loose and crumbling material with a hammer and chisel, exposing the lath beneath the plaster.
2. Wet the area down and fill it halfway to the surface with plaster. Allow this to dry.
3. Wet the area again and, using a plaster trowel, apply another coat of plaster. This time bring the material out flush with the wall or ceiling surface. Allow this to dry.
4. Smooth out the area with a medium grade sandpaper, and patch up defects with spackle. Paint.

One area of a room remains to be patched before painting—wood trim (windows, doors, and baseboards). There is little problem with this. Damage is usually confined to nailholes and minor cracks, which are easily filled with wood putty.

Okay, you are now ready to paint the room. Before doing so, though, you will want to determine how much paint will be needed. Look at the label on the paint can. It will tell how many square feet of surface you can expect to cover with the product. To determine how many

Press fiberglass tape over crack, flatten and then brush on another coat of adhesive.

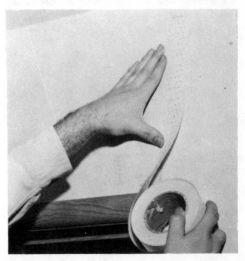

If you don't want to use fiberglass method, use the joint cement-perforated tape method.

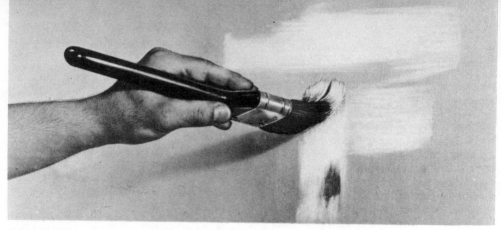

When wall section is refurbished with plug, spot prime wallboard before applying finish.

FORMULAS FOR DETERMINING SQUARE FEET

square feet you will have to cover, use the following:

For ceilings: Multiply the length by width.

For walls: Measure the distance around the room and multiply it by the height of the room. Do not deduct for windows and doors unless these areas exceed 10 percent of the total.

For trimwork: For windows and baseboards, measure the running feet. Allow one pint of paint for each 100 feet. For doors, measure height and width, and multiply.

START WITH THE CEILING

To paint a room, always start with the ceiling. However, if floors are to be sanded for refinishing, do this first to keep dust from flying on to fresh paint. After sanding, cover floors with drop cloths to keep them clear of paint spatter. They are the last area of a room to be coated with a finish material. Even if floors are not to be refinished, protect

If using roller for ceiling, first paint on border area with brush or corner roller.

When painting with roller, be sure to roll paint on slowly to reduce paint splatter.

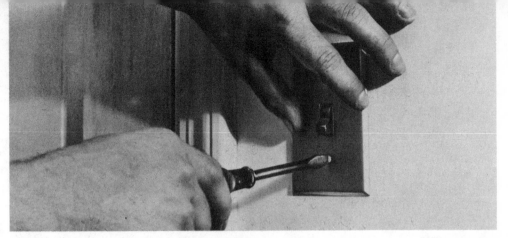

Before you start painting, remove fixtures from wall so your work proceeds unimpeded.

them and furniture with drop cloths. If drop cloths are not available, use newspaper, old sheets, or sheets of polyethylene.

If the surface of the ceiling is not greasy, wipe it down with a brush or rag to remove dust which could dirty the fresh paint. If the surface is greasy, which is a distinct possibility in the kitchen, wash the area with a solution of trisodium phosphate, and rinse with fresh water. Allow to dry before applying paint. This assures good adhesion of the paint which might otherwise start to peel from a greasy surface.

LOOSEN LIGHT FIXTURES

If possible loosen light fixtures and let them dangle. If a light fixture can't be dropped, place masking tape around its edges to keep the fixture from being smeared with paint. Remove other fixtures from the ceiling, such as exhaust fan covers.

The easiest way to paint a ceiling if you are using a paint brush or are hand-holding a roller is to rig up a platform. This facilitates the job and eliminates frequent trips up and down a ladder to shift the ladder. Extend planks, which can be pieces of 2X12 board, between rungs of two stepladders that are positioned at each end of the room. Make sure the plank is strong enough to hold you, and that the legs of the ladders are well braced.

Painting with a roller is facilitated by first brushing on a two inch border around the room's perimeter and attaching the roller to a pole as explained in the second chapter. Figure provides the recommended method to follow when painting a room's ceiling with a roller.

PAINTING WALLS

Painting walls is a simple procedure which doesn't have to be described. However, the job can be made even easier if you observe the following hints:

● Remove all fixtures, such as electrical plates, to avoid having to slow down to "cut in" around them.

● Wipe walls to remove dust and dirt before painting. If kitchen walls are greasy, wash with a solution of trisodium phosphate and rinse with fresh water.

● If trim areas, such as window and door trim, and baseboards, are not to be painted, extra precaution must be taken to assure that they aren't smeared. One of the best ways is to use a cardboard shield, hand-held, when painting near these areas. Hold the cardboard edgewise between the trim and the wall. As an alternative, you can mask off the trim with masking tape. If paint does accidentally get on trim, wipe it off immediately.

If the room is now wallpapered and you wish to have it painted instead, use a latex paint, which provides excellent coverage. If you are painting a kitchen or bath and prefer using an oil-base

When wall plates are removed, you do not have to slow down work to cut around them.

Take your time when painting walls, making sure paint is applied evenly and smoothly.

Make sure trim is firmly in place. You may want to countersink nails and putty holes.

Cardboard makes effective shield to protect areas you don't want to get paint on.

To paint windows, use right brush, and employ shield or masking tape to protect glass.

glossy paint, you will have to remove the wallpaper before painting. Oil-base paint does not adhere to wallpaper. Thus, a wallpaper steamer will have to be used to strip wallpaper from the wall. See "Hanging Wallpaper."

● If wallpaper is to stay in place and will be covered by latex paint, examine the paper for bubbles before painting. If any are found, slit them with a knife, apply some glue to the backside, and press the paper to the wall. Your object is to provide a smooth surface for the paint.

● Whenever you paint indoors, no matter what kind of paint you are using, make sure there is adequate ventilation. Open the windows.

PAINTING THE TRIM

Painting trim involves its own special tricks. After walls and ceilings have been painted, turn your attention to baseboards. To protect the floor, hold a cardboard shield flush against the bottom edge of the trim. Brush paint on evenly and smoothly, using a sash and trim brush. Take your time.

Follow by painting windows. Use masking tape to protect glass. If glass does get smeared, wipe paint away right away before it dries.

Painting window sash is not particularly difficult, but it does require patience. Do it carefully. Figure shows the recommended sequence to follow when painting windows.

Finish the job of painting a room by painting doors and door frames, if you desire them to be painted. Again, the task is simplified by following a correct sequence, which is provided in the accompanying chart.

CHOOSING COLOR

Paint can be very much more than a protective surface covering

The color you paint your house inside or out is a matter of personal choice. If you desire yellow polka dot walls on a purple background, that's your business. You're the one who has to live with it.

However, have you ever stopped to wonder why some color combinations look more pleasing to you than others? For example, I know that when a professional decorator selects colors for a particular room, that room always seems more attractive to me than when a layman selects the colors. Yet, it doesn't have to be this way, because you can employ the same principles of color selection that a decorator uses. Before getting to this, though, let's discuss some of the technical principles regarding color.

Color (or hue) is what the eye sees when light reflects from a surface. The surface itself doesn't have color, but it absorbs some rays emitted by the sun and reflects other rays. The rays which are reflected are the ones that you see.

The basis of all color, then, is sunlight which consists of six colors: red, orange, yellow, green, blue and purple. These intermingle with each other to make an infinite number of combinations.

THE COLOR WHEEL

In determining which color scheme is the one most pleasing for a particular room or for the outside of the house, decorators employ what they call the *color wheel*. This consists of twelve colors: the six sunlight colors and six others made by mixing the six sunlight colors.

To start the wheel, three colors are used. These are the three *primary colors*. They are called this, because from them is mixed every other color. The three are red, yellow and blue, and they are placed equidistant around the circumference of the color wheel.

Next, the so-called three *secondary colors* are added to the color wheel. These are made by mixing equal amounts of adjacent primary colors: yellow and red to produce orange, yellow and blue to make green, and red and blue to create purple.

Finally, a third group of colors called *tertiary colors* are added to the wheel. There are six: yellow-orange, red-orange, red-purple, blue-purple, blue-green, and yellow-green. They are obtained by mixing together equal amounts of adjacent primary and secondary colors.

WARM AND COOL COLORS

Each color on the color wheel is also classified as a warm, cool or intermediate color. Warm colors are those which are

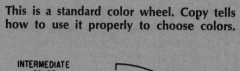

This is a standard color wheel. Copy tells how to use it properly to choose colors.

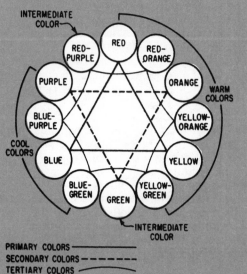

INTERMEDIATE COLOR

RED-PURPLE — RED — RED-ORANGE

PURPLE — ORANGE — WARM COLORS

BLUE-PURPLE — YELLOW-ORANGE

COOL COLORS

BLUE — YELLOW

BLUE-GREEN — GREEN — YELLOW-GREEN

INTERMEDIATE COLOR

PRIMARY COLORS ————
SECONDARY COLORS — — — —
TERTIARY COLORS ‿‿‿

Tints of yellow, orange and gold were used for warmth. Blue-green on chair complements.

associated with fire and sun, giving a feeling of warmth, because they contain red or yellow. Yellow-green, yellow, yellow-orange, orange, red-orange and red are warm colors.

Cool colors are those associated with sea and sky, because they contain blue or purple. Blue-green, blue, blue-purple and purple are cool colors.

Green and purple are neither warm nor cool. They contain sufficient qualities of both classifications to be classified as neither. They are therefore called intermediate colors.

To get a "feel" for working with the color wheel, consider each color as a key on a piano. Strike one, and you get no harmony. Combine two that complement one another, and harmony starts to show through. The more keys you combine, the more harmony you are able to provide if you follow certain rules of harmonics.

The same is true to obtain color harmony. When you combine the colors of the color wheel according to certain rules, you get a harmonious effect. Whether it is the harmony you desire or whether you wish to change "keys" to obtain a different harmony is a matter of taste. But the rules should be followed or the result will be discordant.

COLOR HARMONY

The following is an explanation of how to use the color wheel to obtain certain harmonic effects in your painting:

91

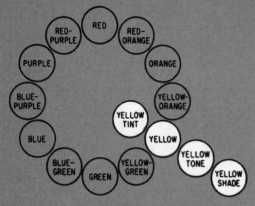

Monochromatic harmony uses one color.

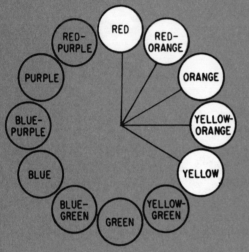

Analogous harmony utilizes related group.

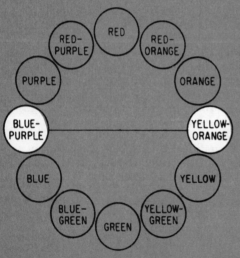

Basic complementary harmony: opposites.

1. *Monochromatic harmony.* This color scheme is the simplest of all, since it involves the use of only one color of the color wheel. The color is varied by varying its tint, tone and shade. Monochromatic harmony, although restful, dignified and unifying, can also be monotonous and dull if displayed over a wide area. Thus, it should be used in small rooms only.

2. *Analagous harmony.* An analogous harmonic color scheme employs colors which are next to each other on the color wheel. Most times three to five colors are employed to achieve a soft and subtle decor which creates an overall warm or overall cool effect.

3. *Complementary harmony.* When a sharp contrast in color is desired—one that gives a vivid, dramatic or gay effect —colors directly opposite each other in the color wheel can be employed. Decorators often use complementary harmony in children's rooms, and play and activity areas. As for other rooms of the house, startling effects can be obtained by using complementary harmony with black and/or white.

4. *Split complementary harmony.* One drawback to the use of complementary harmony is that it may tend to become monotonous. To add "life" and richness of a third color to a complementary color scheme, you can use a base color and two colors than flank its direct complement. Split complementary harmony is one of the most popular methods used by decorators to obtain color schemes.

5. *Adjacent-complementary harmony.* This is a tricky technique, so be careful if you use it. It's a variation of true complements that adds a color from either side of one of the complements.

6. *Double-complementary harmony.* The double-complementary harmony technique provides four colors with which to work by carrying the split complement idea one step further. The two colors on either side of the directly opposite colors are employed.

7. *Mutual-complementary harmony.* To obtain a really colorful effect, use the mutual-complementary harmony treatment. The technique combines the anala-

Walls in action room are covered in blue and white Naugahyde, rosewood panels, shelves backed with mirrors. Bright colors in painting are picked up in quarry tile floor, furniture.

Guest room is tastefully done in antiqued white woods, gold walls, green leaf print.

gous and complementary harmony systems. First choose five adjoining colors from the color wheel. To this, add the complement of the central color. You can go even beyond this and utilize the *split-mutual complementary harmony* technique by adding the colors on either side of the complement to give a total of seven colors. However, keep in mind that there is a point where too much color can be employed. Color combinations utilizing more than three or four colors should not be used in any but very large rooms.

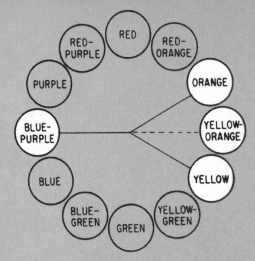

Split complementary harmony is interesting.

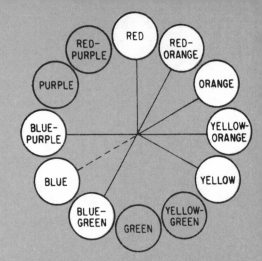

Adjacent complementary harmony is tricky.

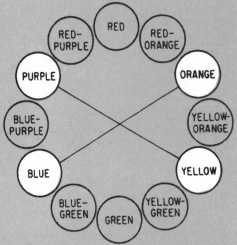

Double complementary harmony is good.
Split mutual complementary harmony.

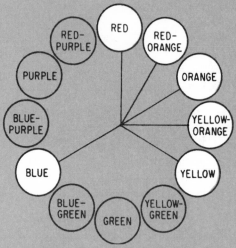

Mutual complementary harmony is colorful.
Triad harmony. Balance the tones carefully.

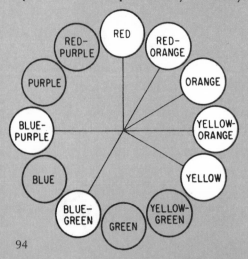

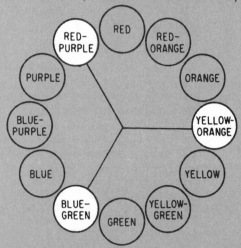

Paint a giant of a house elephant gray and watch it shrink. Lighter entry adds good accent.

8. *Triad harmony.* Used properly, this technique provides for a perfect balance of tones. It utilizes three colors which are equidistant from each other on the color wheel. The technique can be varied in any number of ways by using pure hues, tints, tones or shades of the principal colors.

PRINCIPLES OF PROPORTION

Choosing a color scheme is practically automatic when you employ the color wheel and the techniques just described. However, principles of proportion should be kept in mind. The most pleasing effect is obtained when a disproportionate balance between warm and cool colors is maintained. This is true for all color schemes except monochromatic harmony and analagous harmony, which are employed when special effects are desired. A color scheme should avoid use of opposite colors in equal amounts of light and dark combinations.

How many colors should you use in a room? Three or four is sufficient for an average size room, with more being added in proportion to size as size increases. In considering which colors to put into your house, consider more than a single room. In other words, the entire house should be treated as a color unit. In today's homes, rooms are more open to one another, and there should be a traceable repetition of key colors throughout the house. The technique of color flow throughout the whole house is called *color linkage* by decorators. It would be a good idea to keep it in mind next time you paint.

CREATING ILLUSION

Another thing to keep in mind is that colors can do more for your home than simply create a pleasing effect. Color can give the illusion of creating an architectural change, alter the apparent sun-exposure of a room, and establish the emotional mood of a setting. In other words, color can create an illusion.

In creating a color illusion, there are several basic rules to remember. They are as follows:

1. Warm colors create an illusion of intimacy. They advance toward the viewer visually and give the effect of a room being smaller than it really is while

95

An old house looks smaller and neater in a dark color. Light accents confine attention.

objects in the room appear larger. Warm colors look warm and tend to make a room stimulating and cheerful.

2. Conversely, cool colors back off from the viewer visually and tend to make a room look larger and more spacious. Cool colors look cool, and tend to make a room appear quiet and restful.

3. Light colors expand because they reflect light. Thus, they make a room seem more spacious, and objects in the room seem large but lighter in weight. Light colors are literally cool, because they reflect light. They are cheerful.

4. Dark colors absorb light. They therefore tend to make objects appear smaller, but heavier in weight. Rooms seem smaller and more confining. Dark colors are literally warmer, because they absorb light. They could be depressing if used in excess.

5. Bright colors are those of high intensity. They exaggerate the size of objects, because of their eye-catching char-

acteristics and cause an area to close in upon you visually. Although stimulating and gay, bright colors can be distracting and unrestful if used in excess.

To this point in our discussion of color, we have been concentrating upon the inside of the house. But what of the outside? Need you always use white, for example, because it is the safest to employ or can you go color?

Of course, white doesn't have to be your choice. In fact, you can make color work for you as well on the outside of your house as on the inside. Here are four ways in which it can —

1. Color can help you obtain the maximum value from the design of the house.

2. Color can help give your house a distinctive character all its own.

3. Color can help you blend your house harmoniously in with its surroundings.

4. Color can allow you to correct architectural defects.

Dark roof and deep-toned paint on second floor lowers square house. Accent with dark doors.

Rosewood built-in with dark green walls, gold and green furnishings, dark red accessories.

Beige Calcutta window shades have an orange trim, resemble burlap. Dark wood floor, beams and trim accent terazzo counters and matching floor trim. Cabinets, and ceiling are white.

White walls with black trim and dark accents form perfect background for bright Lees rug in tones of oxblood, red, orange and raspberry. Antique and contemporary mixes well.

Enlarge small door and window openings with built-up trim painted a light accent color.

Where rooms open into entrance foyer, and foyer echoes the exterior colors used on the house, the rooms should be compatible in their color schemes. Consider house as a whole.

Minimize protrusion of small dormers by painting them same color as roof or dark trim.

Large-windowed sun porch uses same or complementary colors as outside of house since the colors will show when drapes and curtains are opened and should not be sour note.

House of many materials can be unified by painting the whole in two tones of same color.

COLOR ACCENTS

If you have an early American or Dutch colonial style, for instance, the projecting second story can be emphasized by painting it a different color from the lower story. If your home has a covered walkway or attractive entrance area, it can be accented with a brighter color than the main body of the house.

Do you have a rambling ranch? If so, its long, low lines can be emphasized with horizontal accents of color. If the house has high windows, such as in bedrooms or utility room, you can use the lower edge of these as a horizontal line projected the length of the house. Upper walls should be painted a different color.

Climate can have an effect upon the color you put on the outside of a home. Pastels and vivid colors, for example, that would be too jarring if employed in climates where they would contrast against a gray sky, are recommended for warm, sunny parts of the country. By contrast, a gray tone is suggested where gray skies prevail for part of the year.

COLOR STYLING

To help you along in color styling your home, consider the following suggestions:

1. Color illusion can work as well on the outside of the house as on the inside, so review the rules outlined above.

2. White and light colors reflect the sun's rays best and actually keep a home cooler in warm weather.

3. Avoid real dark colors except if you have an architectural fault you are trying to hide. Very dark colors near the foundation line, for instance, keep foundation plants and shrubs from showing to best advantage.

4. Don't use accent colors to outline the house like a Christmas tree. Use color judiciously on trim, so it doesn't detract from the main body of the house.

5. Allow fence and garden walls to employ the same accent color you use on the house to tie the house into its setting.

6. Bring outside color indoors once you have established a color character for your house.

SPECIAL INTERIOR PAINT JOBS

Refinishing of hardwood floors and painting of basement areas

This chapter discusses two additional interior refinishing jobs which you may want to accomplish: Refinishing of hardwood floors, and painting of basement walls and floors.

Done carefully and patiently, you can refinish your home's hardwood floors as competently as a professional for much less the cost. The task, which only appears messy and tedious, is not hard at all. If a logical procedure is followed, as explained below, you will end up with excellent results.

RENT SANDING MACHINES

Naturally, the sanding equipment needed for refinishing of hardwood floors are not items you would want to buy. Fortunately, these machines can be rented for a nominal fee from a paint, hardware, lumber or building supply dealer. However, renting of equipment presents a pitfall. If you are not aware of certain facts, you could do work with the wrong kind of machinery, which raises the possibility of doing serious damage to floors.

There are two types of sanding machines—a drum-type and a disc-type. With drum sanders, sandpaper is mounted on a cylindrical drum that rotates on an axis parallel to the plane of the floor and at right angles to the direction in which the machine moves. In other words, the sandpaper cuts in straight lines in the direction of machine movement.

With disc-type sanding machines, the sandpaper is mounted on a disc that rotates in a circle. As the machine moves across the floor, the sandpaper makes spiral scratches which cross the wood's grain. This machine is for someone who has much experience in floor refinishing. Although sanding of floors can be accomplished in a shorter period of time using a disc-type sanding machine, it is not recommended for your use. Inexperience can cause gouging of the sandpaper into the wood floor.

USE A DRUM-SANDER

Therefore, rent a drum-type sanding

Small-sized cracks in floor boards can be filled with plastic wood for finished look.

A flooring nail or two driven into floorboard that squeaks will solve the problem.

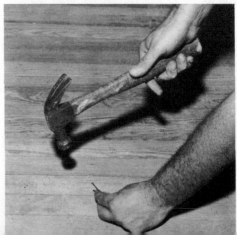

Drum type sanders can be rented. Sheets of sandpaper are inserted into front roller.

machine. In addition, you will also need a disc-edge sander. Another name for this machine is an edger. It allows you to sand off the old finish along the room's perimeter where the sanding machine cannot reach. Although an edger is a rotary machine like a disc-type sanding machine, it does not present the disadvantage of the latter. You have better control over the smaller edger since you hold it by hand and can vary the pressure of the cut.

There are other items of equipment that you will need to refinish a floor. For one, you will need a hand scraper to scrape the finish out of corners where neither sanding machine nor edger can reach. Use of a hand scraper involves elbow grease, but it is recommended instead of a varnish remover. The latter is quite messy and is flammable, which

presents a problem if you like to smoke while working. You will also need various grits of sandpaper and refinishing products, which will be explained as we discuss the refinishing procedure to follow.

FIRST STEP IS IMPORTANT

If nothing else, refinishing hardwood floors is similar to painting in one critical aspect. The most important step for assuring a great job in each case is proper preparation of the surface. If there is one thing to remember when refinishing hardwood floors, it is this: the final result depends on the first step. A refinishing material—shellac, varnish, synthetic varnish—simply covers and protects the wood. It does not level out uneven areas or make rough spots smooth.

Countersink protruding nails before sanding. Nail heads can rip paper in machine.

How you prepare the surface also has a bearing on the type of gloss you will eventually end up with. A brilliant gloss, which most of us want our hardwood floors to have, is created by the reflection of light rays. The smoother the surface, the greater that reflection—the greater the reflection, the greater the gloss. Furthermore, floors which are properly smoothed are much easier to keep clean.

Do not cut corners in preparation, and do not rush the sanding operation. Tests conducted by the Pierce and Stevens Chemical Corporation reveal just how important proper preparation is to the final result.

In one test, a floor panel was sanded with coarse sandpaper only, while another floor panel received the full sanding operation. Finish was applied to both and a 60° gloss meter was used to measure the reflections. The properly sanded panel registered a gloss that was more

Lever raises, lowers sanding machine drum. Never remain motionless, drum-to-floor.

Sand with grain of boards if possible. Two passes in each lane are usually necessary.

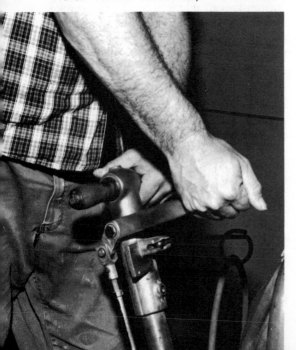

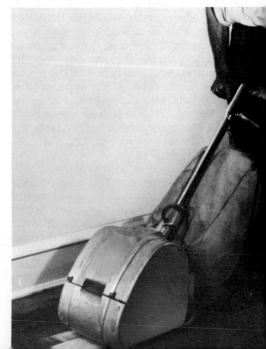

The edging machine employs sandpaper discs. It is a rotary machine with a dust bag.

Rotary edger is okay for sides since good hand control is needed to prevent scoring.

than three times greater than the other panel.

PREPARATION

Before you start to sand a floor, there are several important steps that have to be applied. These are as follows:

1. Wear clean, soft-soled shoes to keep from marring the floor after it is sanded.

2. Remove all furniture, pictures, shades and other furnishings from the room. Anything left on the floor will impede your progress with the sanding machine. Anything left on the walls or over the windows will become dirty from flying dust.

3. Open all windows and close doors to adjoining rooms to dissipate dust and

to keep it from flying into other rooms where it will dirty furnishings.

4. Carefully inspect the floor. Look for protruding nailheads. Countersink these below the surface and fill holes with plastic wood. Allow the plastic wood to dry as recommended in the directions for use before sanding.

5. As you walk across the floor, listen for loose, squeaky floorboards. Drive flooring nails into the board nearest a squeak, slanting the nail at a 50° angle. This will tighten the board and eliminate the squeak. Countersink nails and fill holes with plastic wood.

6. If you spot small-size cracks in or between floorboards, fill them with plastic wood. However, if a crack runs the length of a board, leave it alone. Plastic

Smaller drum sanders, of course, are also useful for finishing off those difficult edges.

Edging machine is also used on stairways. Smaller areas are easily handled by disc.

wood shrinks as it dries. It will not crumble if used to fill smaller cracks. However, it will crumble when spread over an appreciable area, and you can mar a nicely refinished floor with small bits of the material.

By the way, it is not necessary to remove baseboard moldings prior to refinishing. The edger will strip finish from the floor right up to baseboards.

THE SANDING OPERATION

Equip the sanding machine with a 3 1/2 (20-grit) coarse sandpaper. This will remove the old finish down to bare wood. Start at one wall and walk straight ahead to the opposite wall. Move the sander *slowly* over the floor *lengthwise with the floorboards*; that is, with the grain .

Now, walk backwards and pass the sanding machine along the same path. This return pass permits further cutting of the old finish and allows the sander to pick up dust created during the first pass.

Follow this procedure throughout the entire sanding operation. Each complete pass from wall-to-wall and back again should overlap the previous pass by one to three inches.

KEEP SANDER MOVING

This next point is very important: Never stop the forward motion of the sander while the drum is in contact with the floor. If the machine is allowed to rest on one spot, deep cuts, scratches and gouges will result.

All drum sanders are equipped with some means of raising and lowering the drum. However, if by some chance your machine is not equipped with a lever that allows you to control the drum, raising and lowering of the drum is accomplished by tilting the machine backwards or forwards.

PARQUET DESIGNS

If you have a parquet or other block-type of flooring in your home, the indiscriminate pattern makes it impossible to sand with the grain of the wood. In this case, you will have to forget about the way in which grain runs and simply use the sanding machine as described above. However, to minimize the number of scratches, use a 2 1/2 sandpaper for the first cut, which is a finer material.

After making the first cut, turn your

Scraping is needed to get finish off corners since drum and rotary will not reach.

Sweep and vacuum floors, apply finish soon after to seal raw wood and retain efforts.

attention to the edges. Equip your edger with the same grit paper as you used in the sanding machine. Work the machine in a back-and-forth motion over the surface, employing light pressure. Do sanding slowly.

Now, remove the old finish from corners, from beneath and around radiators, and from other areas where the edger can't go. Use a professional hand scraper for floors. These are larger than other scrapers, and have sharp cutting edges that facilitate the work.

THE SECOND SANDING

You are now ready for the second sanding step. The purpose of this is to remove the roughness caused by the coarse sandpaper. Equip your sanding machine with a 1 1/2 (40-grit) sandpaper. Walk at a slow to medium pace passing the sander over the floor lengthwise to the floorboards. Walk forward and then back, as you did during the first pass. Overlap the previous pass by two to three inches.

After completing the main body of the floor, equip the edger with the same grit paper and sand the room's perimeter.

THE FINAL SANDING

The third and final sanding step is essential for obtaining an absolutely smooth surface. Although the floor may look fine after the second sanding step, the last step is necessary for optimum smoothness.

Equip the sanding machine with a 2/0 (100-grit) sandpaper, which is very fine. Pass the sander over the floor, going lengthwise with the floorboards. You can accelerate your walking step, but maintain the procedure of passing over a lane twice and overlapping previous passes by two to three inches.

Finally, sand the perimeter of the room with the edger, which should be equipped with 2/0 sandpaper.

When sanding has been completed, wipe dust from window and door ledges, and other surfaces where you see it. This is done as a precaution. If dust remains and happens to fall on the floor after the finish is applied, the job will be marred. Follow dusting with a thorough cleaning of the floor with a vacuum cleaner. The floor is now ready for the finish, but you have a couple of options available.

Chisel masonry cracks open and fill with a patching material before painting the area.

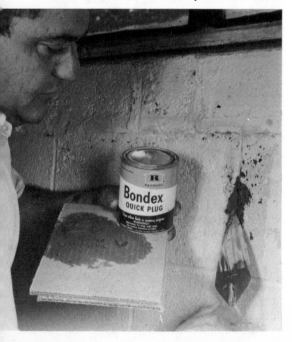

Apply patching material into and around the crack. Trowel smooth and paint over area.

STAIN IF DESIRED

You can leave the wood its natural light, grainy color or you can darken it. If you desire a darker floor, a stain has to be applied before the finish. Any good quality oil stain will suffice. Apply it in accordance with manufacturer's instructions and allow it to dry overnight. Before applying the finish to the floor the next day, rub the stained floor down thoroughly with clean cloths.

The finish coat should be applied as soon as possible after sanding to prevent moisture that is carried in the air from penetrating bare wood. In some cases, as we will discuss below, a wood filler application may be desirable. This goes on before the finish and should be applied as soon as possible after sanding.

If freshly sanded floors are allowed to remain exposed for any length of time, moisture can enter the pores of the wood, causing white spots, chipping, peeling, and premature wear of the final finish when it is applied.

APPLYING THE FINISH

Applying a finish isn't particularly difficult. You do it with a paint brush or roller. However, there are several factors to consider in selecting the type of finish best suited for the needs of your floor. Briefly, a good floor finish should possess the following characteristics:

● It should be hard, tough, and durable to withstand the wear that it is to receive for many years.

● It should be easy to apply and should dry quickly to allow prompt use of the floor.

● It should provide a beautiful and lustrous surface.

● It should be easy to keep clean.

● It should be easy to touch up, so that worn spots, when re-coated, will blend with adjacent areas. If it is difficult to match a finish, you may have to re-sand the entire floor to touch up one small spot that has worn.

Floor finishes fall into four categories: Shellac, varnish, floor sealers, and synthetic resin varnishes. The following are the characteristics of each, which you should consider in making a decision as to which one to use:

SHELLAC

It is the least expensive of all the floor finishes. It comes in either white or orange, but white shellac darkens wood less than orange shellac. In applying shellac, three coats are recommended, with a three-hour waiting period required after the first coat. Following application of the second coat, the floor should be hand sanded lightly. Before the final coat is applied, a waiting period of 12 hours is necessary.

The use of a wood filler before you shellac oak floor is optional. Filler will give the floor a somewhat better appearance, but the effort might not be worth the result. Maple and pine flooring should never be coated with wood filler before shellac is applied.

The chief drawback to shellac is that the finish can soften when too much frictional heat, which is generated by excessive walking over the floor, is created. When the finish softens, dirt and grit eats into the surface and mars the appearance. Furthermore, water dropped on a shellacked floor, unless wiped up immediately, softens the finish and causes white spots. A shellacked floor requires more waxing than other finishes. In fact, some floor experts recommend waxing once a month. It becomes necessary to periodically remove wax buildup on the floor if you expect to retain the floor's appearance. Another drawback of shellac is that the film tends to get brittle with age, which increases the chance of marring and scratching the floor.

To sum up, then, shellac is not recommended for heavy traffic areas or where water is liable to fall on it. If you wish, you can use it in such rooms as a master bedroom.

VARNISH

Shellac and varnish as floor finishes are fairly similar, with the one big difference being that varnish resists water.

However, it too is classified as a "light-traffic" finish. It costs about the same as shellac.

Varnish dries very slowly. Do not use so-called "quick-drying" varnish on floors, because they are less durable than regular varnish.

Since it takes each coat of varnish at least 24 hours to dry, and three coats are recommended, a wood filler should first be applied to oak flooring to protect the wood from dust, lint, and moisture penetration. Allow filler to dry for 12 hours before applying the first coat of varnish. However, never use filler on maple or pine flooring. It is necessary to hand-sand between coats of varnish after the finish has dried. You don't have to sand after applying the last coat, however.

Frequent waxing of varnish-finished floors is recommended. Varnished floors are subject to scratching and marring as the finish ages. Varnish also tends to get progressively darker.

PENETRATING FLOOR SEALERS

This is the finish used mainly by professional floor refinishers. They are acceptable for household floors which get a normal amount of use.

Since the first coat of sealer penetrates into the pores of the wood to protect it against dirt, stains, and moisture, a wood filler application is not necessary. The first coat should be applied liberally and should be allowed to penetrate the wood for about 15 minutes. Then, excess is wiped off with a dry cloth.

Allow the first coat of sealer to dry for about 24 hours. Then, buff lightly with a power buffer equipped with a fine steel wool pad. Apply a second coat of sealer and let that dry for 24 hours. Buff again, and refinishing is concluded.

Floors treated with penetrating floor sealer require regular waxing to protect the wood agsinst abrasions. Depending on how much wear the floor receives, waxing should be done every three to six months.

SYNTHETIC RESIN VARNISHES

As explained in the chapter on "Spe-

Walls must be bare or painted with the same portland cement paint. Wet but do not soak.

Cut in joints in block wall using a stiff-bristled brush, then do surface of blocks.

cial Paints," these are the most durable and most expensive of floor finishes. Unless you have a house full of children and your floors take a great deal of punishment, you will not need this type of finish unless you want to have floors which are virtually maintenance free. No wood filler application is needed prior to applying this finish. Two coats are required, with a light hand sanding needed after the first coat dries, which takes from 15 minutes to 4 hours depending on the type of finish. Allow the second coat to dry for the same period of time.

A floor finished with a synthetic resin varnish seldom needs waxing, except perhaps after the finish is first applied (read the instructions on the can). A dusting with a dry mop or a wiping with a damp sponge is usually sufficient to brighten up the finish. If you use a damp sponge, be certain to wipe up moisture immediately.

Once floors are refinished, you will want to keep them in good condition. One of the things you have to guard against is staining, especially if the floor has been refinished with shellac, varnish, or a penetrating floor sealer. Floors that are coated with a synthetic resin varnish do not stain, because the staining material cannot penetrate the armor-plated finish.

REMOVING STAINS

In attempting to remove a stain from a hardwood floor, always begin the cleaning operation at the outer edge of the stain and work toward its middle. This type of cleaning procedure keeps the stain from spreading. Remember to treat stains as soon as possible after they occur. They are easier to remove.

The following are the more common types of stains that can plague hardwood floors and how to eliminate them:

Dried milk — Rub the stain with a damp cloth. Rub dry and re-wax.

Water marks — Rub the stain with No. 00 steel wool and re-wax. If this fails to clear the spot, sand lightly with No. 2/0 sandpaper and brush away dust. Pour a little mineral spirits or turpentine on the stain and rub the liquid in using No. l steel wool. Let the area dry and apply shellac, varnish, or penetrating floor sealer — whichever finisher was used originally. Feather the edges of the finish as you apply it. Allow the finish to dry thoroughly, then wax.

Heel marks, caster marks — Rub vigorously with fine steel wood and a good commercial floor cleaner for wood floors. Wipe dry and wax.

Ink stains – Rub the area and vicinity with No. 1 steel wool and mineral spirits or turpentine. If the spot persists, sand with fine sandpaper, feathering out into the surrounding area about three to four inches. Rewax.

If the spot still remains, apply a solution consisting of one ounce of oxalic acid to one quart of water. If one application fails to remove the stain, try another. Oxalic acid is a bleaching agent. When used, the treated area will have to be refinished.

Animal and diaper stains – Spots which aren't too old can be treated the same as ink stains. If the spot resists cleaning, sand the area with No. 00 sandpaper and apply a matching finish. Let the finish dry and buff lightly with No. 00 steel wool. Apply a second coat of finish, allow to dry, and wax.

Chewing gum, crayon, candle wax – Lay some ice on the spot until it becomes brittle enough to scrape off. In addition, pour a little cleaning fluid around the area (not on the spot) and allow it to soak beneath the substance. This will help loosen it.

Cigarette burns – If the burn isn't too deep, rub the spot with a piece of steel wool which has been dampened in water. – Rub with a liquid or paste wax, silver polish, boiled linseed oil, or a cloth slightly dampened with ammonia. Re-wax.

Oil and grease – Rub with dry kitchen soap that has a high content of lye. Or, place a wad of cotton which has been saturated with hydrogen peroxide over the stain. Saturate another wad of cotton with ammonia and place it over the first wad. Repeat the process until the stain disappears.

PAINTING MASONRY

The various kinds of masonry paint and uses of each are discussed in the chapter on "Special Paints." However, there are several precautions that must be taken before paint is applied. These will assure a long-lasting, excellent paint job.

Regardless of the paint you use, clean the surface. Use a wire brush to remove dirt, loose particles, and other foreign matter which will interfere with paint adhesion. If you see white salt-like deposits on the concrete, stucco, or mortar, it is probably efflorescence, which is caused by moisture that dissolves salts in the interior of alkaline materials and carries them to the surface. Efflorescence must be removed before painting. This can be done with a wire brush.

Remove grease or oil by washing with a proprietary cleaner available at a paint dealer or with ordinary detergent and water. Now, if efflorescence is *not* present and if you are *not* using a water-thinned paint, such as latex or portland cement paint, wash the surface with water and allow to dry.

PREPARATION

Before you start to paint, double check these important points –

1. If the surface is well aged (one to two years of exposure to the elements), chances are that most of the alkali has been washed out or neutralized by the atmosphere. You have no problem on this score and do not have to treat the surface for alkali prior to painting. However, age increases the possibility of contamination by dirt, oil, and grease. Therefore, make absolutely certain your cleaning job is thorough.

2. If the surface has been previously painted, use a wire brush to remove loose material. However, if the surface is very poor, and the old paint is loose, peeling or heavily chalked, you will probably have to sandblast to remove all old paint before repainting.

3. If you are applying a water-thinned masonry paint over old paint that is in fairly good condition, use a surface conditioner to assure complete adhesion of the new paint over the old. This conditioner is a penetrating sealer type and is available from your paint dealer.

4. Read the instructions on the can of masonry paint you are going to use and follow them carefully. No one knows better than the paint manufacturer what his product can and cannot do, and what precautions must be taken with it.

SELECTING WALLPAPER

You can decorate, enhance, change visual sizes, even cover up

Many homeowners prefer to use wallpaper in certain rooms of their homes rather than paint, or they may wish to combine the two, using one or the other for accenting a wall of a particular room. Since wallpaper is as important to a home's decor as paint, the subject has a place in this book.

The one thing which strikes one about modern wallpaper is the fact that in most cases it can be handled competently by the homeowner—even one who has never before hung wallpaper. Credit for this must go to the wallpaper manufacturers, who are now making products so accurate that paper can be hung with a minimum of measuring and cutting.

WALLPAPER OR PAINT?

Before discussing the various kinds of wallpaper you will be able to buy, and distinguishing between those which the inexperienced homeowner can handle and those he shouldn't attempt to hang himself, let us discuss the advantages wallpaper has over paint. These can be summed up as follows:

Wallpaper offers a wider choice of decorative selections. There are literally hundred of patterns and colors from which to select.

Wallpaper can cover surface irregularities much more effectively than paint. However, wall damage must be repaired as discussed in the chapter on "Interior Painting" since irregularities can appear through the wallpaper surface.

Wallpaper can make a room seem larger than it really is. A vertically stripped paper, for instance, hung in a room which has a low ceiling makes the room seem higher. A horizontally stripped wallpaper applied to the walls of a room which is narrow makes the room seem wider.

EASY TO HANG

Most wallpapers are produced by ma-

The pattern of one roll of wall covering will coincide exactly with other rolls.

Wall coverings offer wide choice of colors and patterns which paint cannot hope to do.

Easy-to-clean vinyl wall coverings cannot be harmed by soap and sponge scrubbing.

Some wall coverings are pre-pasted and come in water box which is filled before hanging.

chine. This assures that the pattern of one roll will coincide perfectly with other rolls of the same pattern, facilitating cutting and hanging. This was not the case several years ago. Nor is it the case today with expensive handprinted papers, which the homeowner should not attempt to hang himself unless he has experience. These handprinted products are very expensive and much more difficult to hang than regular type wallpapers.

In previous days, wallpaper was made with a 1-to-1 1/2 inch blank border edge (selvege) that protected the paper during shipment and storage. If the paper was accidentally crushed enroute to the dealer or while lying on a shelf in the store, the blank edge, not the pattern, would receive the punishment. When the paper was being made ready to hang, selvege had to be cut off. If cutting wasn't done carefully, the paper would appear to be hanging crooked. Cutting of selvege was a tedious, difficult task.

Today's wall coverings are shipped in heavy containers that protect them. There is no selvege. The paper is removed from the container and hung. Modern wallpapers are strong, durable, and easy to keep clean.

MOST ARE NO LONGER "PAPER"

Oddly, most wall coverings today are not wallpapers in the technical sense of the term. Wallpaper is a paper material, which may or may not be coated with a clear, wash-fast plastic that allows cleaning with a damp sponge. The material, like its predecessors, is thin and difficult to manage while it is being hung.

Products that are being sold now, although still referred to as wallpaper, are composed of a vinyl on a fabric (not paper) backing. They are heavier than ordinary wallpaper, which makes them easier to handle. They are also extremely simple to keep clean. You can scrub

Humidity doesn't harm vinyl wall coverings. They are also mildew and fungus resistant.

vinyl-fabric coverings with a damp sponge and soap.

SOME ARE PRE-PASTED

Some vinyl-fabric coverings come pre-pasted. These require a dampening with water before you can hang them. Just wet the back and hang, like a postage stamp. However, adhesion to the wall is not as firm or as assured as vinyl-fabric wall coverings to which you apply paste.

Vinyl-fabric wall coverings are moisture resistant, and you can hang them in rooms where there is a high concentration of humidity, including baths and kitchens. Ordinary wallpaper cannot stand up under humidity and will begin to crinkle and peel from a wall. They are designed for use in rooms where there is little or no humidity.

REMOVING FROM WALLBOARD

In addition to being fire, mildew and

ROOM ESTIMATING CHART

Distance Around Room in Feet	Single Rolls for Wall Areas Height of Ceiling			Number Yards for Borders	Single Rolls for Ceilings
	8 ft.	9 ft.	10 ft.		
28	8	8	10	11	2
30	8	8	10	11	2
32	8	10	10	12	2
34	10	10	12	13	4
36	10	10	12	13	4
38	10	12	12	14	4
40	10	12	12	15	4
42	12	12	14	15	4
44	12	12	14	16	4
46	12	14	14	17	6
48	14	14	16	17	6
50	14	14	16	18	6
52	14	14	16	19	6
54	14	16	18	19	6
56	14	16	18	20	8
58	16	16	18	21	8
60	16	18	20	21	8
62	16	18	20	22	8
64	16	18	20	23	8
66	18	20	20	23	10
68	18	20	22	24	10
70	18	20	22	25	10
72	18	20	22	25	12
74	20	22	22	26	12
76	20	22	24	27	12
78	20	22	24	27	14
80	20	22	26	28	14
82	22	24	26	29	14
84	22	24	26	30	16
86	22	24	26	30	16
88	24	26	28	31	16
90	24	26	28	32	18

This chart will help you to estimate how much wall covering you need for a room. It is based on a single roll covering 30 square feet of wall area.

Today, many of your modern wall coverings are of vinyl flocks on a fabric backing.

fade resistant, vinyl-fabric wall coverings can be stripped. Ordinary wallpaper must be steamed or scraped from a wall when you redecorate a room. Vinyl-fabric coverings, on the other hand, can simply be pulled from the wall. However, there is a precaution you should follow. If the material is hung on gyspum wallboard, there is danger of pulling away the wallboard paper surface with the wall covering. This is true except in the case of a covering which has a synthetic fiber backing, which we will discuss below. Thus, you would be safer to use a wallpaper steamer or hot water to loosen the wall covering from the wallboard.

Vinyl wall coverings are available with several types of backings. These backings fall into three distinctive categories, as follows:

NON-WOVEN FABRIC

This is the oldest type of backing which supports a vinyl face. Frankly, the material is only slightly heavier than ordinary wallpaper of good quality. The pre-pasted type of wall covering mentioned above is available with a non-woven back only.

WOVEN FABRIC

This material feels like cloth and is as strong. You can hardly rip a covering that has a woven fabric back. Coverings made in this manner require paste when hanging. However, because of the material's weight, it is easy to handle, and wrinkles and airpockets are minimized.

Class for class, wall coverings with both non-woven and woven fabric backings are more expensive than ordinary wallpaper. Taking 500 square feet of wall as an example, cost of decorating with the fabric coverings is from $65 to $100. Vinyl-coated wallpaper will cost $10 to $45. Ordinary wallpaper, without a vinyl coat, will cost as little as $7.50.

SYNTHETIC FIBER BACKING

As of this writing, wall coverings with a synthetic fiber backing are the newest

Vinyl wall coverings are safe for the kitchen. Hot grease and food wipes off easily.

types available. The backing consists of a mixture of cellulose, latex, and rayon. One of the major advantages of this covering is that if you make a mistake while hanging the material, you can pull it from the wall and rehang it without fear of wrinkling or destroying the material. In all other respects, a vinyl surfaced wall covering having a synthetic fiber backing possesses the advantages of a non-woven fabric wall covering.

VINYL WALL COVERINGS

When decorating with a vinyl wall covering, there are several important points to keep in mind. These are as follows:

● If you are decorating a basement or patio where moisture may come into contact with the backing, select a covering which requires hanging with paste. Paste contains an anti-mildew compounds, which will protect the covering from fungus.

116

Modern wall coverings can be stripped when you wish to remove them without steaming.

the room. This material is made of polypropylene olefin fiber, which is spot and stain resistant. The material can be used in all rooms, including kitchen and bath. It will not support mildew or rot. You clean this covering by vacuuming with a vacuum cleaner.

Carpet squares are easily installed. They come with a special adhesive supplied by the manufacturer or with a double-faced tape.

Another type of covering, which is easy to install and keep clean, are 12-inch square panels of pure vinyl tile. These won't scratch or stain, and are easily kept clean with a damp cloth. They are self-adhering and can be trimmed with a razor blade.

Similar to vinyl tiles are rigid panels of vinyl that simulate brick and cut stone. They are self-adhering, and there is enough in a box to cover 12 square feet of wall.

ROLL-ON DECORATIONS

A new type of "wall covering" that you paint on is actually a roller that has decorative embossments over its surface. As you roll paint on the wall, the decoration appears. It works similar to a car that rolls in a puddle of paint, leaving a clear design of its tire pattern on the road.

FINALLY — ARMORED VELVET

Other than these types, there is one other wall covering that should be mentioned although the homeowner cannot apply it himself. This covering consists of solid-colored nylon pile which is shot into a coating of epoxy adhesive with an electrostatic gun. It is called Armored Velvet, and provides a room with a degree of sound conditioning and insulation as well as decor.

The material can be applied to any type of base, including masonry, glass, wood, and metal. It is impervious to dirt, which is easily vacuumed from the surface. Neither will it support stains, fire, nor mildew. The covering is the most expensive available, selling for as much as $2 per square foot.

● Avoid metallic pigmented patterns. As of this writing, this type of fabric has a tendency to fade in rooms which receive direct sunlight.

● Always check the covering you select for durability. Rub a swatch with a cloth to determine if the pattern will rub off.

● After wall coverings are hung, remove dirt and stains promptly with a mild detergent, a clean sponge or soft brush, and a water rinse. Never use abrasive cleaners. Wash an area that is larger in size than the stain to avoid leaving a ring.

OTHER TYPES

Besides those wall coverings mentioned, there are other types you can buy. One is carpet tile, which are 12-inch squares of carpeting that you can lay on the floor and extend over the wall if you wish to carry a design throughout

Hang the strip from the ceiling allowing a slight overlap. Cut the overlap off later.

HANGING WALLPAPER

Prepare the surface and follow these simple steps to success

There is nothing very difficult about hanging wallpaper providing you follow the five steps a professional takes. These are:

PREPARE THE SURFACE

Wallpaper should be applied to a smooth, clean surface to assure proper adhesion and insure that wall irregularities won't show through the surface. Generally, cracks and holes should be filled, and rough spots and small bumps should be sanded. For a complete dis-

cussion of how to repair surface irregularities, see the chapter on."How to Prepare and Paint Rooms."

If there is wallpaper now on the wall and it is loose in spots or shows other signs of damage which could affect the new material, it should be removed from the wall. The best way is with a wallpaper steamer, which can be rented from a paint and wallpaper dealer. This is an electrically operated machine that ejects a spray of steam that will penetrate the pores of the wallpaper and loosen paste holding it. If you cannot take advantage of a wallpaper steamer, soak the old wallpaper with hot water, and keep applying hot water until the paper loosens.

If old wallpaper is firm and tight, there is no reason why you shouldn't hang new paper right on top.

If you are hanging wallpaper on top of a painted wall, and the paint which was used is oil-base, wash the wall with trisodium phosphate to dull the gloss. Gloss will prevent maximum adhesion of the paper to the wall. Be sure to rinse the wall with clean water after the trisodium phosphate bath.

Allow the wall to dry and brush on a liberal coating of wall size. This material, which is granulated glue, serves two purposes: it fills small depressions left in the wall and prevents the wallpaper's edges from coming loose and curling; and it facilities removal of wallpaper in the future if you wish to take it from the wall.

By the way, if the wall is new — never been painted or papered — apply an interior primer paint. Follow with an application of wall size. Then, you can proceed to hang wallpaper.

MEASURING AND DROPPING A PLUMB LINE

Start at a corner. Measure in from the corner to a distance which is one inch *less* than the width of the wallpaper. For instance, if the wallpaper measures 24 inches, you measure in from the corner along the wall to a distance of 23 inches. You do this to provide a one inch overlap around the corner and on to the adjacent wall when the first strip is hung.

Drop a plumb line from the ceiling to the baseboard along the mark and snap a chalk line down along the wall. Measure the height of the wall from ceiling to baseboard and measure off the first strip of wallpaper. Make sure it is approximately 3 inches longer than the ceiling-to-baseboard height. Cut the strip from the roll.

A plumb line down the wall can be marked or snapped to provide vertical first guide.

If paper was rolled too tightly and curls, unroll few feet and pull over table edge.

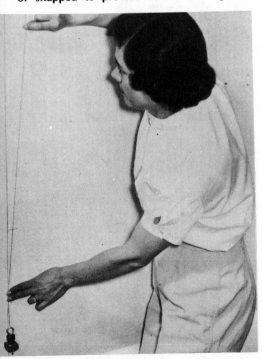

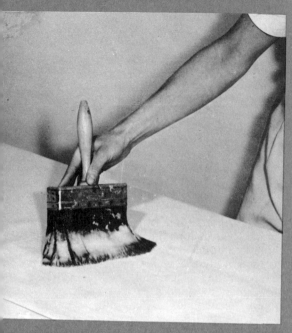

Apply a liberal amount of paste to back of paper, paying particular attention to edges.

Fold the paper toward the center, wet side to wet side so that the edges butt together.

When paper is straight, pull open bottom fold and brush firmly down and to sides.

Trim areas to be removed with sharp knife. Scraper blade holds paper, provides edge.

Succeeding strips are butted against last strip hung. Each strip will follow first.

When hung, this first strip—the so-called reference sheet—will overlap the corner by one inch and will overlap the ceiling-wall joint and baseboard. Each strip of wallpaper you cut henceforth should also overlap ceiling-wall joint and baseboard, but not necessarily the corner of the room.

Keep one extremely important point in mind regarding the reference sheet. It must be hung absolutely straight, so take your time. If this strip of wallpaper is straight, you can be sure that succeeding strips will also be hung straight.

PASTING AND HANGING

Apply paste to the back of the first strip of wallpaper. Make sure you cover it fully and with a liberal amount. Many times, edges are inadvertently missed or not coated thoroughly enough. Pay particular attention to these areas.

Now, fold wet side to wet side toward the center of the strip for the top and bottom edges butt together. Being careful not to crease the paper, carry it over to the wall. Start at the ceiling. Pull open one folded end and hang the strip so its outside edge lines up perfectly with the chalk line you snapped. Make sure the top overlaps the ceiling-wall joint. Now, gently pull open the other edge and place the bottom half against the wall, overlapping the baseboard.

SMOOTHING AND TRIMMING

As you unfold the paper and apply it to the wall, use a wallpaper smoothing brush as a squeegee to smooth out the paper. Apply firm pressure, making sure

At corners, use your brush edge hairs to poke paper firmly into corners for good fit.

To insure a tight seam between strips, use wallpaper roller. First check for bubbles.

that no air pockets remain. You can locate air pockets by running your hand over the surface, feeling for lifted areas. If you find any, run the smoothing brush over them. At the corner or around door and window casings, actually pound the paper into place with the brush bristles. Paper at these points, and also at ceiling-wall joint, must fit tightly.

To trim excess wallpaper at the ceiling and baseboard, crease the paper into the joint with the back of a pair of shears. Pull the paper carefully away from the wall and cut along the crease line with the shears. Press the paper back into place and smooth.

There is an alternate way of trimming excess. Use a metal straight edge to crease the paper at the joint and remove excess with a sharp razor blade or wallpaper cutting wheel. However, be certain that the blade or wheel is very sharp. A dull tool can tear the paper. If you use a razor blade, have several on hand since two or three cuts dull a blade's edge.

Incidentally, if you plan to hang a border strip along the top (or bottom) of the paper, at ceiling or baseboard, you don't have to be too careful when trimming the edges at these points. Border strips are usually two inches wide and will cover imperfections made by cutting.

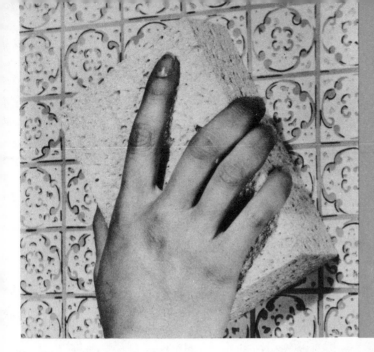

When the first wallpaper strip is hung straight and smooth, begin to cut succeeding strips. Begin by matching up the pattern of the next strip with that of the reference strip. Be sure to leave the overlap at ceiling-wall joint and baseboard as you did with the reference strip.

Before hanging the second strip, match it up with the pattern on the roll of paper and cut a third, fourth and fifth strip — or as many as are needed to finish the wall. Apply paste to all, folding each end to the center as before. Pre-pasting strips in this manner allows the paper to absorb paste and shrink before being hung. Now, begin to hang succeeding strips, lining up on the reference strip. As you apply strips, make sure that joints butt together. Do not overlap them. To assure a tight seam, push the edges together carefully by hand and then roll the seam with a wallpaper roller.

Never skip areas, such as around doors and windows, intending to return to them later. Hanging wallpaper is a continuous operation. You hang each strip in turn, covering each area as you come to it, and smoothing and trimming each strip. If this caution is not followed, a patchwork quilt effect might be the result.

As you come to corners, allow the wallpaper to fall into place around the corner in a natural fashion *unless* it overlaps on to the adjacent wall by more than two inches. In this case, assure a tight corner crease and cut the paper along the crease. Wallpaper that extends around a corner by more than two inches has a tendency to buckle.

WASHING

As each strip of wallpaper is hung, wash it down immediately with a sponge saturated with water. Never use a rag. It could leave marks on the paper. The purpose of washing each strip is to remove dirt, finger marks and excess paste. Washing also helps to keep the paper from wrinkling as paste dries.

If paper begins to "bubble" in a spot or two after you have applied it, air is trapped beneath or you missed an area with paste. Smooth bubbles if possible with the wallpaper brush. If this doesn't help, allow the bubbles to remain in place for a couple of weeks. Often, a bubbled area will begin to adhere to the wall.

However, if none of these procedures work, slit the bubble with a sharp razor blade. Work a little wallpaper paste beneath the paper with an eyedropper. Press the paper firmly back into place.

Simple, flat-painted walls are sometimes a necessity when you wish to dramatize prints.

GLOSSARY OF PAINTING TERMS

A

Abrasion—The wearing away of paint film by some external force.

Acrylic—A monomer or polymer which is characterized by good durability, gloss retention, crystal clarity, and color retention.

Adhesion—The sticking together of substances in contact with one another.

Aging—Permitting a material to stand for some time and grow old.

Agitator—A paint mixer.

Air dry—The ability of a coating to dry to its ultimate hardness under normal atmospheric conditions.

Alkali—A soluble salt which is the opposite of acid. It has the ability to neutralize acid. Also called *base*.

Alkyd—The chemical combination of alcohol, acid, and oil. Alkyd is widely used as a vehicle for paint.

Alligatoring—A paint film failure that resembles an alligator skin or a dried out river bed.

Anodizing—An electrolytic surface

treatment for aluminum which builds up an aluminum oxide coating.

Asphalt — A black resin or gum that occurs naturally or can be derived from petroleum.

Atomization — The breaking up of paint into finely divided tiny droplets, which is usually accomplished in spray painting.

B

Base — A colored or white paste or heavy liquid added to paints to tint them and to which is added a vehicle to make a finished paint.

Binder — That part of a paint which holds the pigment particles together, forms a film, and imparts certain properties. It is usually a polymer and is also called *vehicle solids*.

Bleeding — The property of some paints to transfer their color upwards into topcoats which are applied over them. Diffusion of coloring matter through a coating from a substrate.

Blistering — The formation of bumps or pimples on a paint film. Blistering is normally caused by moisture or heat.

Blushing — Hazing or whitening of a film caused by absorption and retention of moisture in a drying paint film.

Body — The consistency of a liquid.

Brittle — Lack of flexibility, usually combined with a lack of toughness.

Bronzing — The formation of a metallic appearing haze on a paint film.

Brush — An applicator for applying paint.

Brushing — The act of applying paint by a brush or the ability of a paint to be applied by a brush.

Butadiene — A petroleum derivative capable of forming polymers such as artificial rubber.

Butyl acetate — A solvent for paint that is commonly used in lacquers.

C

Carbon black — A black pigment manufactured from carbon.

Carbon   — A toxic solvent generally used for cleaning.

Casein — A component of emulsion paints.

Castor oil — A natural vegetable oil used in the manufacture of alkyd resins and as a plasticizer.

Catalyst — A component that speeds up a chemical reaction without entering into the reaction.

Caulking — A sealant used to seal joints and prevent the passage of a fluid, usually moisture.

Cellulose — A natural polymer, generally of wood or cotton.

Chalking — A result of weathering of a paint film that is characterized by loose pigment particles on the surface of the paint.

Check — A paint failure characterized by small cracks on the surface of paint film.

Clear — A paint containing no pigment or only transparent pigments.

Coating — The act of applying paint or the actual film left on a substrate by a paint.

Coconut oil — A natural vegetable oil used in the manufacture of alkyd resins.

Cohesion — A molecular attraction by which the particles of a body, whether like or unlike, are united together throughout a mass, such as a paint film.

Color — The visual appearance of a material.

Color retention — The permanence of a color under a set of conditions.

Compatibility — The ability of two or more materials to mix together to form a homogeneous mixture.

Concrete — An alkaline substrate requiring special paints.

Condensation — A change from a vapor to a liquid on a cold surface.

Consistency — The fluidity of a system.

Copolymer — A polymer made from two monomers.

Coverage — The amount of area a volume of paint will cover at a certain thickness.

Crawling — A wet film defect which results in the paint film pulling away from certain areas or not wetting certain areas, leaving those areas uncoated.

Crazing — A film failure that results in

surface distortion or fine cracking.

Curing — The chemical reaction which takes place in the drying of paints that dry by a chemical change.

D

Degradation — The gradual or rapid disintegration of a paint film.

Degreasing — Cleaning a substrate (usually metallic) by removing grease, oil, and other surface contaminants.

Density — The weight of any material per unit of volume.

Dipping — Applying paint to an article by immersing the article in a container of paint and then withdrawing the article and allowing excess paint to drain from the part.

Dispersion — The act of distributing solid particles uniformly throughout a liquid. Commonly the dispersion of pigments in a vehicle.

Drier — A catalyst added to a paint to speed up the cure or dry.

Dry — The change from a liquid to a solid which takes place after paint is deposited on a surface. Included in drying is the evaporation of the solvents and any chemical changes that occur.

Durability — Length of life. The term usually applies to a paint that is used for exterior purposes.

E

Emulsion — A suspension of fine polymer particles in a liquid. The dispersed particles may be binder, pigments or other ingredients.

Enamel — Usually a pigmented gloss paint.

Epoxy — A class of resins characterized by good chemical resistance.

Ester gum — A hard brittle resin used in lacquer.

Evaporation — The change from liquid to a gas. When solvents leave a wet paint film, they do so by evaporation.

Evaporation rate — The speed with which a liquid evaporates.

Extender pigment — An inert, usually colorless and semitransparent pigment used in paints to fortify and lower the price of pigment systems.

Exterior — The outside. An area not protected from the weather.

F

Fading — Loss of color.

Fatty acid — An acid derived from a natural oil.

Filler — A heavily pigmented paint used to fill imperfections or pores in a substrate.

Film — A very thin continuous sheet of material. Paint forms a film on the surface to which it is applied.

Flag — The split end of a bristle in a paint brush.

Flaking — A paint failure characterized by large pieces of the paint falling from the substrate.

Flat — Lacking in gloss.

Flexibility — The ability of a paint film to withstand dimensional changes.

Flow — The leveling characteristics of a wet paint film.

Fungicide — An additive for paint used to prevent the growth of mold or fungus in the container or on a dry paint film.

G

Gloss — The ability of a surface to reflect light.

Gum — A solid resinous material which can be dissolved and which will form a film when the solution is spread on a surface and the solvent is allowed to evaporate. An ingredient of varnishes.

H

Hardness — That quality of a dry paint film which gives the film resistance to surface damage or deformation.

Haze — The development of a cloud in a film or in a clear liquid.

Hiding power — The ability of a paint film to obscure the substrate to which it is applied.

Holiday — An area which was accidentally missed when a surface was painted.

House paint — A pigmented paint designed to be applied to the exterior surfaces of residences.

Hue — The characteristic by which one color differs from another.

Humidity — The amount of water vapor in the atmosphere.

I

Inhibitor — An additive to a paint which slows up some process, such as yellowing, skinning, etc.

Iron — A metallic substance which requires painting to prevent corrosion.

L

Lacquer — A paint which dries by solvent evaporation only.

Latex — An emulsion. A dispersion of a polymer in water.

Lead — A metal commonly used in the manufacture of driers and pigments.

Lifting — The attack by the solvents in a topcoat on the undercoat which results in distortion or wrinkling of the undercoat.

Lightness — The whiteness of a paint.

Light fastness — The ability of a paint to resist color changes caused by light.

Linseed oil — A vegetable oil widely used in the manufacture of alkyd resins and also as a binder by itself.

Luster — Gloss.

M

Mildew — A fungus growth which appears on substrates in warm, humid areas.

Mixer — Any container that contains an agitator.

Moisture — Water vapor or liquid.

Monomer — A chemical compound, usually simple, capable of reacting with itself or other monomers to form polymers.

Mottling — A film defect appearing as blotches.

O

Oils — Commonly vegetable oils. Obtained from various natural sources. A relatively viscous liquid which has a slippery feel. Used as modifiers for alkyd resins, as paint vehicles, as varnish constituents and as plasticizers.

P

Paint — A substance that can be put on a surface to make a layer or film of white, black or colored material.

Pastel — A light color. One containing much white.

Peeling — The loss of adhesion of a paint film which results in large pieces of film splitting away from the surface.

Phenolic — A class of resins, which are characterized by good chemical resistance.

Phenylmercury compounds — A class of materials used as fungicides.

Pigment — An insoluble solid having a small particle size. Incorporated into paint system by a dispersion process. Used to color paints.

Plasticizer — A material that is added to a paint system to make the film more flexible.

Polymer — A chain or network of repeating units combined chemically. Formed from monomers by polymerization. For example, polyvinyl acetate is a polymer formed by hooking together of many vinyl acetate units. Vinyl acetate is a monomer.

Polymerization — The formation of a polymer from monomers. The two types of polymerization are addition and condensation.

Primer — The first coat of paint which is applied to a substrate. It is often the most important coat for controlling such things as corrosion, adhesion loss, blisters, etc.

PVA — Polyvinyl acetate.

R

Resin — A solid or semi-solid material, usually polymeric, which deposits a film and is the actual film-forming ingredient in paint.

Retarder — A solvent added to paint to reduce the evaporation rate.

Rust — The corrosion product which forms on iron or steel that is exposed to moisture.

S

Sagging — Excessive flow on a vertical

surface resulting in drips and other imperfection on the painted surface.

Sanding — The smoothing of a surface with an abrasive paper or cloth.

Semi-gloss — An intermediate gloss level between high and low gloss.

Sheen — The gloss or flatness of a film when viewed at a low angle.

Shellac — A natural gum that is useful in the manufacture of certain types of paint, chiefly lacquers. Also a solution of this natural gum which is widely used to paint hardwood floors.

Silking — Lines in a paint film resultfrom the draining off of excess paint in a dip or flow coating process.

Skinning — The development of a solid layer on the top of the liquid in a container of paint.

Solids — The percentage, on a weight basis, of solid material in a paint after the solvents have evaporated.

Solvency — The measure of the ability of a liquid to dissolve a solid.

Solvent — A liquid that will dissolve something, commonly resins or gums or other binder constituents.

Spar varnish -- A clear varnish that is useful for use on surfaces that are exposed to the exterior.

Spray — Application of a paint by spraying.

Stabilizer — Something that is added to paint to prevent degradation.

Substrate — The piece or object that is to be painted.

T

Tack — The stickiness of a paint film.

Thinner — One or a mixture of several solvents or diluents that are used to reduce the viscosity of paint or to lower the solids.

Tint — A very light color. Also, to add color to another color or to white.

Titanium dioxide — A white pigment that has the greatest hiding power of all white pigments.

Topcoat — The final layer of paint applied to a substrate.

Turpentine — A solvent obtained from the distillate of the exudation of pine trees.

U

Ultraviolet light — That portion of the spectrum which is largely responsible for the degradation of paints.

Undercoat — A first coat, primer, sealer, or surfacer.

Undertone — That color of a pigment which shows up when that pigment is mixed with much white pigment.

V

Varnish — A clear resin solution made by the application of heat to a mixture of hard gum and a vegetable oil, and then dissolving the product formed in a suitable organic solvent.

Vehicle — All of a paint except the pigment.

Vinyl — A class of monomers which can be combined to form vinyl polymers. Characterized by their toughness, flexibility, and durability.

Viscosity — The resistance to flow in a liquid. The fluidity of a liquid. For example, water has a low viscosity and molasses has a very high viscosity.

W

Weathering — The changes caused in a paint film by natural forces, such as sun, rain, airborne dust, etc.

Wetting — The process by which a liquid forms intimate contact with the substrate to which it is applied.

Wrinkle — The pattern formed on the surface of a paint film by improperly formulated coatings. The appearance of tiny ridges or folds in the film.

Y

Yellowing — A discoloration to the yellow, which is commonly caused by smoke, grease, certain gases, and sunlight.

Z

Zinc chromate — A yellow, rust-preventing pigment useful on steel.

Zinc oxide — A white pigment that is useful in preventing mold or mildew on paint film.

INDEX

Index Key:

Chapter heads are in capital letters